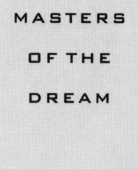

MASTERS

OF THE

DREAM

MASTERS OF THE DREAM

The Strength and Betrayal of Black America

ALAN L. KEYES, PH.D.

WILLIAM MORROW AND COMPANY, INC.

NEW YORK

It is the policy of William Morrow and Company, Inc., and its imprints and affiliates, recognizing the importance of preserving what has been written, to print the books we publish on acid-free paper, and we exert our best efforts to that end.

LIBRARY OF CONGRESS CATALOGING-IN-PUBLICATION DATA

Keyes, Alan L. (Alan Lee), 1950–
Masters of the dream : the strength and betrayal of Black America
/ Alan L. Keyes.
p.   cm.
Includes bibliographical references and index.
ISBN 0-688-09599-2
1. Afro-Americans—Race identity.   2. Afro-Americans—Social
conditions—1975–   I. Title.
E185.625.K49   1994   305.896'073—dc20   94-28840   CIP

Printed in the United States of America

First Edition

1 2 3 4 5 6 7 8 9 10

BOOK DESIGN BY BRIAN MULLIGAN

To Mom and Dad

ACKNOWLEDGMENTS

I must first recognize the indispensable contribution from Martin Gross. He first suggested that I make a book out of my thoughts about the black American experience, and introduced me to the folks at William Morrow. I appreciate the cooperative spirit of Morrow editor Bob Shuman, and of Zach Schisgal, who took charge of the project at Morrow when Bob moved on.

I have to thank my good friend Dave Shapinsky for his help in pulling together some of the initial research materials, and for many hours of conversation during which I argued out and tested some of the ideas this book presents. I am also grateful to Alvin Williams for helping me to think about ways to make my ideas accessible to a younger generation of black Americans. I also benefited from Paul Rahe's comments and suggestions, and Charles Lichenstein's reactions to the early chapters.

My friend and lifelong teacher, the late Allan Bloom, taught me to see and respect the relationship between freedom and moral character. He has obviously had a fundamental influence on all my work. My writing owes a lot to the patient ear and clear thinking of my true soul brother, Marlo Lewis, to whom I read aloud from almost every page. I offer affectionate thanks to Robin McElhaney, who has been the mainstay of my working life for many years, and to Jay and Dee Parker who, like my own parents, strengthened and supported my spirit. I thank my children, Francis, Maya, and Andrew, for knowing when to leave their dad alone and when to offer him some comfortable distraction. Jocelyn, my wife, knows better than anyone the emotional effort it took to write some parts of this book, and without her understanding and forbearance I could not have accomplished anything.

I am grateful as well to those like the Reverends Jim and Jean Thompson, and Peter and Starr Parker, who offered their encouragement and prayers for the success of this project. Like all of my people, in the end I owe everything worthwhile in my nature and life to the Creator and his Divine Providence.

CONTENTS

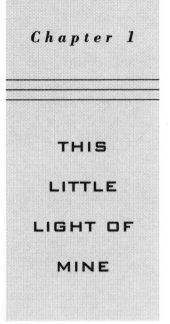

Chapter 1

THIS

LITTLE

LIGHT OF

MINE

T he American dream is dead. That's what we're being told today by supposedly insightful sociologists and media pundits.
We're seeing the first generation of young people who can't expect
to do as well as their parents did, they say. They won't have as nice
a home, or drive such a nice car, or work a job that pays as well.
The dream is dead.

One premise of this book is that these conclusions miss the
mark. They are based on a misconception. The American dream
wasn't just about money and material advancement. It was a dream
of freedom. Tycoons and stockjobbers weren't its only heroes. They
were also colonists from Europe who traded houses and jobs in
developed cities and towns for the hardship of life in a wilderness.
They were families who exchanged comfortable city life in the East,
for a dangerous westward trek in covered wagons across the Plains.
They were men who died thirsting in the great American desert
and women who gave up frills and fancy dresses for days working
their fingers to the bone. Most of these people weren't guaranteed
a better future in material terms than the one they left behind.

Some sought riches, to be sure. But others sought the right to worship God in their own way, or to build communities in which they themselves could make the decisions and the laws. Pioneers like Daniel Boone or Abe Lincoln's father gave up farms in settled communities to move farther west, where they could, as the saying went, breathe free.

It was a dream of freedom. And its heroes included Native Americans who fought against overwhelming odds to maintain their autonomous way of life. They included fugitive enslaved blacks who braved the tracking dogs and bounty hunters to follow the North Star out of slavery. They included the enslaved blacks these left behind, who, following the North Star of their faith, never surrendered the kernel of their humanity or their hope for a better day.

To those who limit their vision to the dingy materialism that passes for ambition in our day, it will seem strange to assert that black Americans are the masters of the dream. Were we not enslaved, then banished by racist discrimination from the precincts of economic advancement? We were. As enslaved people, we African Americans could not legally claim to own even our own bodies, much less the fruits of our bodily labor. When slavery formally ended, discriminatory segregation stunted our educational opportunities, and confined most of us to menial, low-paying jobs. If the American dream is mainly an economic result, black Americans had little or no part of it. But if the dream includes the longing for freedom, or the values and character that make people capable of it, then the enslaved and their offspring can indeed lay special claim to be its masters.

Thanks, though, to the triumph of a materialistic conception of the dream, much of the heritage that justifies this claim has been forgotten or denied. We hear all about black poverty and deprivation. We hear little about the rich spiritual values or the strong qualities of mind and heart forged by our hard experience. We hear about the young men in prison, the unwed mothers, the broken families. We forget about the *majority* who, over the decades, married, worked hard, and held families together against all odds.

We can ill afford to continue this neglect. Already, generations of black children have grown up without any sense of their true heritage. Consciously or unconsciously, their minds are influenced by those who, for whatever reason, spread the doctrine that racists ripped black Americans from our African roots, stripped us of our values and institutions, and left us with no shred of our own culture or humanity. Leaders like Louis Farrakhan, who claim to be strong enemies of racism, have taken this demeaning doctrine as a major premise of their creed. Ironically, in order to prove the worst in others, it requires that we deny the best in ourselves.

This doctrine has its roots in the long-prevalent, and still popularly accepted, notion that slavery dehumanized African Americans, wiping out all traces of the enslaved's African past.

During capture and passage, the process of dehumanization began, and once in slavery the transition to property was complete. The American slavery system, unlike any other arrangement in the history of civilization, was unique in its absolute insistence on the "subhumanness" of its victims.[1]

The Negro slaves in the United States were converted from the free, independent human beings they had been in Africa, to property. They became chattel. This process of dehumanization started at the beginning of the slave-gathering process and was intensified with each stage along the way.[2]

American slavery destroyed the household gods and dissolved the bonds of sympathy and affection between men of the same blood and household. Old men and women might have brooded over memories of their African homeland, but they could not change the world about them. Through force of circumstances they had to acquire a new language, adopt new

habits of labor, and take over, however imperfectly, the folkways of the American environment. . . . Of the habits and
customs as well as the hopes and fears that characterized the
life of their forebearers in Africa, nothing remains.[3]

These statements may accurately describe the intent of the
American slave system. But should we assume that the slave system
achieved its purpose? Does the fact that their white captors regarded and treated blacks as subhuman chattel mean that enslaved
blacks became what their captors' laws and attitudes intended them
to be? For a while, historians and other students of slavery simply
accepted these assumptions without question. They studied the
slave system primarily through the eyes, and from the perspective
of the enslavers. As early as 1941, however, Melville K. Herskovits
produced *The Myth of the Negro Past*, a pioneer anthropological
study of the survival of African traits in the language, habits, and
beliefs of black Americans. But it was not until the 1960s that
scholars began in earnest to debunk the myth that racist oppression
destroyed African-American culture and humanity.[4] In the preface
to his monumental history of the world of the enslaved, Eugene
Genovese aptly summarized the general conclusion warranted by
this research:

> Many years of studying the astonishing effort of black people
> to live decently as human beings even in slavery has con-
> vinced me that no theoretical advance suggested in their ex-
> perience could ever deserve as much attention as that
> demanded by their demonstration of the beauty and power of
> the human spirit under conditions of extreme oppression.[5]

Nothing deserves more attention, yet nothing has been more
shamefully neglected in discussions in the media or on the political
stage. When we talk about issues involving race or conditions
among blacks, the old debunked stereotypes of blacks as dehu-

manized victims still prevail, even among black leaders who surely should know better by now. The problem is that the truth about black values, virtue, and character doesn't fit the victim's role that black Americans have been forced to play in order to justify constant expansion of the bureaucratic welfare state. It doesn't fit the passion play of absolute annihilation and national redemption a leader like Farrakhan evokes to appeal to black anger. It doesn't fit the assumption of a white monopoly on traditional virtues that underlies the too-narrow national vision of some conservative thinkers and politicians.

Most tragically, though, it doesn't fit the secret shame felt by many blacks themselves when they remember their heritage of bondage and subjection. Most African Americans are the descendants of enslaved people. Slavery is therefore a part of our backgrounds and, whether we consciously admit it or not, a part of each individual's identity. When black people read about the enslaved, or see them depicted in movies or on television shows, we invariably feel that their experiences belong to us as well. But what does this really mean? Consider, for example, the following passage from a formerly enslaved person's remembrance of his childhood:

Nights, I allus slept by Missus' bed. Daytimes, my bed was push' up under her'n. Dis was called a trundle bed. She kept me right wid her most ob de time, an' when mealtime come she put me under de table an' I ate out ob her hand. She'd put a piece ob meat into a biscuit an' hand it down to me. Den, she say, "When dat been finished, holler up after some more, Ike." But she allus warn me not to holler if dere been company to dinner. She'd say, "Jes' put you' hand on my knee an' den I'll know you is ready." But seem like my mouth been so big, an' I eat so fast, an' only Mis' so busy talkin' to dem ladies, dat I jes' keep a-touchin her on de knee, most ob de time.[6]

Of course, children, fed under the table like puppies, became adults who could be beaten in the fields like wayward dogs:

> A woman who gives offense in the field, and is large in the family way, is compelled to lie down over a hole made to receive her corpulency, and is flogged with the whip, or beat with a paddle, which had holes in it; at every stroke comes a blister. One of my sisters was so severely punished in this way, that labor was brought on, and the child was born in the field. This very overseer, Mr. Brooks, killed in this manner a girl named Mary; her father and mother were in the field at the time.[7]

Slavery was infuriating and degrading.[8] What black person can read a passage like this without once again feeling the anger, but also the degradation. Somewhere, therefore, in the consciousness of every African American there is a subtle temptation to disown our captive ancestors, and to think that our past is not a triumph to be celebrated, but a shame that we must overcome. Influenced by this feeling, we may have been all too willing to accept interpretations that invite us to look beyond or away from our heritage of captivity when seeking the foundations of our ethnic identity. So we look to Africa, glossing over the fact that Africa is not home to a single, united people but to a polyglot diversity of tribes and nations.[9] The Africans who came to America probably didn't think of themselves as Africans until they had been here for a while. If today African Americans have a common ethnic identity, it is not something that was brought from Africa and preserved. It is something that emerged from and on account of our American experience, especially the experience of slavery.[10] Our common identity owes much to our shared experience of oppression, but it owes much more to the moral and spiritual resources that made it possible to survive in spite of it.

The enslaved had no recognized possessions, no achievements

.that he could truly claim as his own. Outwardly, he derived his identity from his captor,[11] and his worth was what he could fetch on the auction block. He could not be his own man. We assume that he existed for his captor's sake, and we see him only from his captor's point of view. He was the victim of a system that denied his humanity. When we think of him, we unconsciously adopt the assumptions of that system. As a consequence, we also deny his humanity. Otherwise, we would be able to see that the enslaved had his own moral purposes and aims, which the slave system conditioned but did not define.

Past efforts to reflect upon these purposes have focused mainly on rebellion and escape. But these, too, are purposes and aims defined entirely by the enslaved person's relation to the slave system. However frequently and decisively we prove that the enslaved never ceased to resist, ever sought to escape and rebel, we will still not have understood what he cared for in himself, apart from the system that oppressed him. Yet unless we treat human beings as ends in themselves, we show no respect for their humanity. As such, the slave is an instrument, like a hammer or a saw, with no worth apart from the task he or she performs, i.e., no intrinsic worth. Thus, ironically, even efforts to illustrate the courage and character of our enslaved ancestors have adopted the dehumanizing perspective imposed by the slave system.

In order to escape this perspective, we have to follow the methods of the enslaved themselves. Forced to survive in a world where their captors dominated all material things, they found refuge for their humanity in the spiritual and moral strength that is the surest sign of humanity. Outwardly compelled to accept their captor's judgment that race and bondage made them an inferior species, they inwardly nurtured the certain conviction that, by the standards of the truer moral universe, they stood in worth far above their oppressors.

We cannot move back in time. Nor can we see into the minds of those enslaved people. But we can glimpse their moral world through the folk tales, songs, and religious beliefs that survived the era of captivity. Often clothed in the language and imagery of biblical faith, they speak clearly of a realm beyond bondage, a home over Jordan where sinners find punishment and righteous souls find peace. In the captor's world, the enslaved is judged only for his material worth, as a possession. But in the moral world, the enslaved preserves a sense of intrinsic worth by holding both himself and his captor to a moral, rather than material, standard. In the moral realm, there is a clear identity between freedom and moral righteousness. In the realm of the wicked, the just are enslaved, but in the moral realm, they are, by virtue of their righteousness, forever free. In the realm of the wicked, the captor's power denies the enslaved's liberty. But not in the moral realm. There, freedom depends upon God's judgment, and therefore upon moral worth rather than material possessions.

The enslaved person's awareness of the moral world nurtured the existence of an inner being, not subject to the vicissitudes of enslavement. Only when we appreciate the existence of this inner person, whose place was determined by a moral, rather than material order, do we begin to understand how the enslaved's humanity survived the elaborate system devised to deny and extinguish it. From childhood, many enslaved blacks understood that slavery contradicted their essential being.[12] They knew that, despite the evidences of worldly power, they had an intrinsic worth and dignity that did not depend upon the captor's judgment. It could not be degraded by the captor's vices, or humiliated by his contempt. Whatever outrages he visited upon them, they could by their own acts of kindness or courage merit far greater respect than the people who violated God's law by enslaving them. Torn from parents and siblings, they could maintain a sense of family ties and obligation. Encouraged to respond only to physical self-gratification, force, and fear they could answer as well to compassion, loyalty, and courage. However much the slave system limited their outward freedom, they could nonetheless retain their capacity for moral choice and action.

What made this moral resistance possible was the belief, born mainly of religious faith, that all individuals possess a divine spark that they can keep alight in every circumstance of life. It did not matter whether, in the eyes of the world, they were enslaved or free, rich or poor, in high position or low. By nurturing and respecting this intrinsic potential, they could be equal or superior to every situation. This source of inward dignity meant that, despite slavery, discrimination, and repression, black Americans as such did not surrender spiritually. This was the key to the survival of the race when the enforced laws and vicious practices of the land might have led to extinction.

As they contemplated the mass of uneducated, desperately impoverished freed blacks after the Civil War, some white observers confidently predicted that, by the next century, few if any blacks would still be alive in the United States. Even some sympathetic whites doubted the ability of the freed blacks to endure.[13] Because of the community's strong basic values, black Americans disappointed these grim expectations. Generation after generation learned and passed on the emphasis on religious faith, strong family bonds, and education—as ends in themselves, and as the means to self-improvement and self-respect. These values made it possible for us to develop and maintain a strong communal life within the boundaries enforced by racist segregation. They made it possible for us to endure poverty without losing our sense of self-worth; to remain powerless without losing the sense of responsibility for ourselves and our families. Our values made it possible for us to build and maintain institutions, such as the family and the church, that would, when the time came, enable black people to strike telling blows for true freedom.

In the backgrounds of blacks prominent in the nineteenth or twentieth century, we can discern the ingredients that composed the strength of the black community. Most drew upon the example and guidance of a parent or other family member for the first foundations of their moral identity. Thanks to these influences, the sense of pride and self-worth was not an abstraction, but a practical instinct. A strong-willed father might be the source of discipline, the goad to courage or hard work. A watchful grandmother or aunt might first suggest that learning is the key. A mother's patient perseverance, relying on the will of God, might lay the strong foundations of religious faith. From each and all of them, a young man or woman would acquire the sense that each individual's actions reflected well or badly on the race as a whole. That meant that every day, in every walk of life, each black person carried an added burden. He acted not for himself alone, but for all members of his community.

In generations past, I doubt that any black American entirely escaped this sense of communal obligation. Blacks lucky enough to enjoy special opportunities for education or advancement were, of course, singled out as models of, or for, the community. But those who lived and labored in obscurity knew they were singled out as well, whenever they ventured beyond the boundaries of the physical and social enclave in which racism confined them. Being black meant, of necessity, being held responsible for the black community. In a negative sense, that was and is the meaning of racial prejudice. To prejudiced eyes, one's race is everything; the individual, nothing. When a white bigot sees a rowdy black person he doesn't think, "That man is rowdy." He says, "Those blacks don't know how to behave." Before the individual has any chance to declare himself, judgment is passed, limits are set, results are predetermined. The individual naturally resents this predisposition, and seeks ways to assert the truth of his uniqueness. He may even try to deny that his communal identity has any role at all in determining his individual personality.

This negative fact has a positive counterpart, however. Prejudice limits and confines the individual, but it also sets him apart. Each black person could feel that he represented the condition of the entire community. Pride was not confined to the favored and successful few. Nor was the sense of responsibility. As individuals, therefore, blacks carried within them a strengthened sense of the community's presence, of the effect that its condition had upon them, and that their actions had upon it.

The black individual was therefore not an atomized, disconnected body. He was everywhere haunted by membership in the group, and he was, at every moment, answering for its existence. The negative effects of prejudice left him with an intense thirst for individual distinction. But his sense of group responsibility implied a powerful communal consciousness. This special combination of individual drive with a sense of collective responsibility is one of the distinguishing marks of black-American character. It represents in the moral and psychological sphere the mixture of group empathy and improvisation we find in jazz, as well as in the interplay between verse leader and congregation that often appears in Negro spirituals and gospel music. The marriage of rhythm and highly individual melodic line in black popular music reveals the same distinctive personality. Community is the rhythm, the reality never far from mind, the truth never completely removed from consciousness. Like rhythm, it provides the defining context for the individual's solo performance. The result of this mix is an individual ambitious for himself, but unable to conceive of himself entirely apart from his community; someone who can work with single-minded drive and discipline in order to improve herself, but who also feels a compulsion to place her achievements upon the altar of communal betterment.

Historically, the black family and the black church nurtured and expressed this special brand of individualism. Both developed as instruments of everyday endurance and resistance under the slave system, despite destructive opposition and manipulation. It was the family and the church that provided the setting in which black Americans evolved their autonomous moral culture and passed its complex substance from one generation to the next. They shaped the extraordinary character that stirred and transformed America's conscience during the Civil Rights movement. They helped to inculcate the sense of intrinsic personal worth that made it possible for black Americans to experience the depravity of racial injustice and systematic abuse without being debased by it.

This last may have been the most important of all. Prolonged injustice can provide a handy refuge for moral weakness and degeneracy. Among black Americans, racial discrimination prevented many men and women from succeeding, no matter how hard they tried. But it could also provide a convenient excuse not to try at all. For most people, life involves a constant internal battle between inclination and obligation. The decisions involved may be no more earthshaking than whether to stay at the bar for another drink, or go home and have dinner with the kids; whether to stay in bed for a few more hours, or get up early to go looking for a job. When people have reason to feel that they are systematically abused, resentment, anger, and self-pity can give self-destructive impulses an edge in these everyday crises of will and determination. It can become all too easy to suppose that the wrong they suffer relieves them of responsibility for the wrong choices they make. In this way, little by little, the sense of personal responsibility can break down until, by degrees, people become the most efficient instruments of their own destruction.

From slavery times until the present, black families and churches helped people to resist this insidious effect of oppression. How they did so is one of the most important things we have to think about here. We know already, from bitter experience, what happens when these crucial institutions can no longer play their vital role. The terrific crisis that literally threatens the lives of millions of people in our urban communities shows us the consequences. The failure to pass on the values that helped black Americans to survive not decades, but several centuries, of mistreatment is taking an awesome toll, especially among the young.

In many urban neighborhoods today, random murder stalks the streets. The stray bullets of gang clashes and drug-related executions claim the lives of infants and passersby. Teenagers gun each other down in drive-by shootings; they stab each other in school hallways. A walk across the street or an errand to the drugstore can lead to a face-off with death.

These urban war zones are less real for most Americans than the action they see on their local movie screens. Yet the brutal TV images of passersby being pulled from their cars and beaten senseless during the Los Angeles riots may foreshadow our entire society's future unless we find a way to bring the covert warfare in our cities to an end. Left unchecked, disorder subverts freedom, as it did in Weimar Germany. People reach a stage where they not only tolerate but demand the use of ever more forceful measures in the effort to quell lawless behavior. I believe this was the psychology of the Rodney King jury. But new levels of force may only provoke new levels of criminal violence. The day may come when we send in the National Guard only to find that we cannot safely withdraw them. If we ever reach a time when we must permanently mobilize military forces in order to contain the simmering violence in our urban centers, our democratic way of life will be radically transformed. Standing armies are dangerous to freedom, especially when they're standing on street corners.

Though we Americans naturally take comfort in thinking otherwise, most violence arises from moral rather than economic causes. Rich people and poor people can live side by side for generations without war and violence, if individuals are secure in their moral identities. But when some feel their identity threatened, the fear that results engenders hatred, which leads to violence. This is one reason why religious, ethnic, and racial differences are still at the root of the world's most intractable conflicts. It is why most wars persist long past the point where their cost in lives and property has surpassed any economic gain either side could hope to obtain from them.

The riots that broke out in Los Angeles in the wake of the Rodney King verdict illustrate this point. For several days, citizens in the afflicted L.A. neighborhoods looted, trashed, and burned businesses that provide jobs for their community. Some were simply thugs and criminals who saw a chance to loot and took it. About 40 percent were employed people, many of them ordinarily decent folks, who later repented for their excesses and even returned the goods they had stolen. It's too easy to assume that these rioters acted irrationally, destroying the businesses that symbolized what they needed and wanted most. It makes more sense to assume that what they destroyed, and what they rioted about, symbolized what they hated most: outside influences, outside powers, and the fact that outsiders dominate every aspect of their lives. This domination leaves no space for them to assert themselves and their own identity. Not only the jobs they work and the businesses they patronize, but the streets they walk upon, the schools they attend, even the places in which they live compel them to live in terms of values, concepts, and goals that appear to be determined by outsiders.

Because those rioters control nothing and have power over nothing, nothing in their environment reflects their own image. Because they see themselves in nothing, it is not long before they see nothing in themselves. And it is not long again until this emptiness itself becomes their identity. The self becomes an antiself, a moral vacuum that sucks all meaning and significance from the things and people around it. Caught in its vortex, people feel themselves to be worthless beings in a world of worthless beings. If anything matters at all, it is only for the moment, and for the immediate sensation that allows them to claim each moment as their own: Sex is a moment, feeling and being felt; death is a moment, killing and being killed; life is a moment that drugs can intensify, until you slam into the concrete truth that each moment of sensation, however intense, provides no lasting foundation for your identity. That truth alone endures, forcing a quest for ever more intense experiences that culminate in hopeless ecstasy or ruthless violence.

In its most explicit form, this moral vacuum spreads under the aegis of the criminal empire that overshadows lost neighborhoods in many of our cities today. It is a world where intensity takes the place of meaning; where the existential rush of becoming blinds people to the possibility of living beyond the moment. It is a world where instinct replaces thought, narrowing the difference between life and death to the thin edge of sensual perception. It is the world of illicit drugs, random murder, and dispirited sexual depravity.

The fact that many urban neighborhoods are gripped by this moral dissolution does not mean that all the people who live in them have given up the struggle against it. On the contrary, many have not. They work. They have families.[14] They try to raise children. But they are the unarmed inhabitants of a free fire zone, caught in the open between the criminals and the police. At the individual level, these people are still strongly motivated to take responsibility for themselves. But almost nothing in their environment offers them the opportunity to extend this sense of responsibility to the community in which they live. As individuals, they resist moral collapse; as a community, they are powerless against it.

All Americans should be deeply concerned about this urban nightmare, but black Americans have reason to be especially distraught. The maelstrom is consuming black youths in greatly disproportionate numbers—the males dead or imprisoned, the females isolated, dependent, and exposed to both physical and psychological abuse and degradation.[15] Why is this happening? When a people has passed through hell and survived to curse the devil, why should they suddenly collapse just as they push aside its open gates? Can the answer be racism or economic deprivation? If so, how do we explain the fact that our ancestors endured racial and economic abuse that was arguably greater and more systematic than we face now, yet managed to resist self-destructive moral disintegration of the type that is killing our people today? Maybe they had something we don't have, or understood something we no longer understand. Maybe we took a wrong turn somewhere that strayed from the paths and precepts that made it possible for us to be in the storm so long, and live to sing about it.

Before dismissing these possibilities, we should consider the fact that most of the physical mayhem blacks are suffering in our cities today is self-inflicted. The young black men dying on the streets aren't being lynched by white racists; the pregnant young women aren't being raped by white captors. Blacks are killing each other, drugging each other, sexually abusing each other.[16] Believe if you like that it's all the result of an elaborate white conspiracy to eliminate black people. If you listen to the talk shows on black radio stations, people invariably call to suggest this explanation. "The white man is bringing the drugs into this country. The white man is bringing the guns into this country. The white man is out to get us." So they say, making it sound like a wonderfully astute discovery. Homey don't think so. Black people were hunted, bartered, bought, and sold by whites for more than two centuries. We were squeezed into slave ships by white slavers to live for months in our own filth with hardly room to breathe. We were beaten and sexually abused by white captors. We were forced to work without compensation. We were lynched, cheated, segregated, and discriminated against by our white fellow citizens. With such a history before us, does it really take years of course work and a Ph.D. to conclude that some whites may be out to get us? If they're not, why did they go to all that trouble?

Just for the sake of argument, let's assume for a moment that the conspiracy theories are true, that whites are behind the drug plague in our neighborhoods. They are conspiring to sell poison to black people, especially young ones. Let's also admit, for the sake of the argument, that a lot of blacks are helping them, sacrificing their brothers and sisters in order to satisfy their cravings for riches, power, and pleasure. As black people considering ways to deal with the problem, we could spend our time trying to discover and somehow overpower the white fomentors of the conspiracy, or we could spend our time trying to defeat the cravings that drive black people to prey upon each other. Which is more within our power?

If we knew enough about it, we might imitate the wisdom of our ancestors. Caught in the solid vise of slavery, they knew that there was little hope of physically overpowering the slave system. But by developing their own moral system, they prevented it from totally overpowering them. Did the slave system attack the idea of the black family? Enslaved blacks cherished it. Did the slave system deny them education? Enslaved blacks valued it highly. Did the slave system seek to abuse their sexuality for profit and secret gratification? Enslaved blacks nonetheless respected the emotional bonds it forged between black men and women. As their first step in defending against the system that abused them, they rejected the system of values it applied to them.

As a system of values, slavery was the ultimate form of economic determinism. It rested on the assumption that blacks had no value except their economic value. They were worth only what they could fetch on the auction block. The key to rejecting the slavery system of values was to reject this economic determinism, and to substitute for it a value system based on the intrinsic worth of each human being in the eyes of God. The ethical tenets of Christianity provided the ideal basis for this alternative system of values. However much the enslavers tried to pervert Christianity into a dogma of mindless obedience to authority, blacks themselves perceived and developed its revolutionary antislavery implications. First in songs, then in sermons, and finally, in public speeches and tracts, they made the point that if all human beings belong to God, they can't legitimately be owned by one another. How can you be sold on the auction block if God is the only one who has the price?

The rejection of the slavery system of values was the key to the survival of black self-esteem, despite the degrading vicissitudes of life in bondage. No matter how thoroughly people were deprived in material terms, an act of kindness, courage, or simple compassion could signal their true worth. Moral action requires no equipment beyond the will to do what is right. Even if we fail, the goodwill and faith revealed in the attempt certify the quality of our lives. No matter how great the physical power that another has over us, we can always preserve our moral autonomy and with it, our self-respect.

The Christian ethical system made it possible for enslaved people to understand that true freedom, moral freedom, was something their captors could not take away. For the enslaved man or woman, the moment of real personal emancipation came with the willingness to assume moral responsibility for their own actions, when they realized that, even in bondage, it was up to them to decide between good and evil. The process of Christian spiritual rebirth represented this moment of insight in religious terms. In order to be born again in baptism and received into the Church, individuals had to recognize and come to terms with their own moral capacity. They had to reject the slave system's implied link between being enslaved and being an inferior person. They had to realize that, before their most important judge, their status depended on their own choices, and was not a necessary consequence of their enslaved condition.

Against the economic determinism of the slavery system of values, the enslaved blacks asserted the idea of intrinsic worth and personal moral autonomy embodied in the Christian worldview. Of course, in the context of the American Revolution and its aftermath, this assertion had a powerful secular counterpart. The theory of human rights and political legitimacy on which the American Declaration of Independence was based translated the key Christian ethical precepts into the concepts and language of political discussion. The idea of intrinsic worth becomes the self-evident truth that all human beings are created equal. The idea of moral autonomy becomes the key principle of self-government: that is, to be legitimate, government must be based upon the consent of the governed.

Blacks who wrote and spoke against slavery, and later against racial discrimination and segregation, developed a rhetoric that amalgamated the principles of Christian ethics with those in the Declaration's theory of human rights. This culminated in the powerful speeches that shall forever immortalize Martin Luther King, Jr. But King's statesmanship went beyond effective rhetoric. The strategy he adopted for the Civil Rights movement took the idea that moral responsibility is the basis for true freedom and made it the touchstone for a revolutionary campaign to overthrow America's system of racial injustice. His doctrine of nonviolence called upon black Americans to display the rich moral character quietly nurtured through the years beneath the surface of material deprivation. It required that the supposed victims of oppression take moral responsibility not only in the struggle for justice, but in the effort to preserve social peace during the struggle.

During the period that culminated in the passage of the 1964 Civil Rights Act, Martin Luther King's statesmanship epitomized the deepest values of the black-American tradition. But after the first great victories over the legal and political structures of racial injustice, black leaders shifted their attention to the economic plight of the black community. They argued that years of economic discrimination, educational neglect, and social abuse had left black people unfairly disadvantaged. They demanded that something be done to repair the damage.

At the level of simple retributive justice, they had a point. Black people *had* suffered injuries resulting in lost earning power and assets, as well as other material damages. Perhaps some way could have been found to quantify the damages and fix the terms for reparations, as the Congress did with the Japanese interned during World War II. Instead, the demand became the basis for a surfeit of analyses and government programs in which economic deprivation became the chief determinant of individual identity. Under the guise of helping them overcome economic disadvantage, blacks were asked to accept the fundamental premise of the slavery system of values—the idea that economic status determines the quality and worth of human life.[17]

By accepting this idea, black leaders surrendered the key bastion of black survival in America. Traditional black values, deeply rooted in Christian ethical principles, supported the ability to resist the materialistic standards of human worth that could damage black self-esteem and corrode the sense of moral responsibility. Abandoning that tradition, liberal black leadership delivered blacks, and especially poor blacks, into the hands of a government-dominated social-welfare network. This system, like slavery, demands, as the price of admission, that blacks surrender to a value system based on economic determinism. As a result, a large segment of the black community appears to belong to a permanent underclass composed of inferior, worthless human beings who are in no position to take responsibility for their own decisions and actions.

The concept of the permanent underclass ought to set off a warning in the minds of black Americans even vaguely familiar with our history. It's a new term for describing the same old situation. Under slavery, blacks were part of a permanent underclass from which even free blacks could not escape. During the "Jim Crow" era, laws were passed aimed at making blacks part of a permanent underclass, separate and unequal. The genius of contemporary social-science jargon is that it manages to present as a simple fact of life what came across in the past as an intentional result. Analyses and policies that in the past might have been construed as a conscious antiblack strategy can be presented today as an empirical response to the intractable character of the permanent underclass. These analyses often include and perpetuate the same negative stereotypes that formed the basis for the conscious and overt antiblack strategies of the past. But the supposedly empirical character of modern social science makes it much harder to criticize them for it.

Consider, for example, the concept of class. William Julius Wilson stirred praise and controversy some years back when he published *The Declining Significance of Race*, in which he suggested that class was more important than race as a factor in determining "black chances for occupational mobility." He concluded that

> it would be difficult to argue that the plight of the black underclass is solely a consequence of racial oppression, that is, the explicit and overt efforts of whites to keep blacks subjugated, in the same way that it would be difficult to explain the rapid economic improvement of the more privileged blacks by arguing that the traditional forms of racial segregation and discrimination still characterize the labor market in American industries. . . . To say that race is declining in significance, therefore, is not only to argue that the life chances of blacks have less to do with race than with economic class affiliation but also to maintain that racial conflict and competition in the economic sector—*the most important historical factors in the subjugation of blacks* [emphasis added]—have been substantially reduced.[18]

As Wilson notes in the epilogue to the second edition, his book "generated vigorous, sometimes heated, discussions of race and class in the black American experience . . ." In the midst of all the heat, people missed the essentially circular reasoning involved in Wilson's argument. He says that his definition of class

> follows closely the conception of class originally developed by Max Weber, with its emphasis on the social relations of exchange. In other words, classes are defined in terms of their relationship to other classes within the market where different commodities are bought and sold and where people with various resources (goods, services, or skills) meet and interact for purposes of exchange.[19]

Using this definition, he develops indices based on the role people play in the economy—for example, occupational titles. Using these indices, he presents a raft of statistics purporting to show a relationship between "class" (economic position) and "life chances" or "chances for occupational mobility" (economic position). Practically speaking, what does this say to the members of the supposed permanent underclass? It says, "Your economic chances depend on your economic status. If you have nothing, you'll get nowhere." This is neither a true statement, nor a helpful one. It's not true because it ignores the possibility that factors having nothing to do with either race or economic status contribute most significantly to economic success. It's not helpful because it encourages poor people to believe that there's no route out of poverty until (by some miracle they can't influence) their economic status improves.

A female lawyer will generally earn more money than a woman on welfare, and her children will have better "life chances." But is the significant factor in this difference the lawyer's income, or the values of discipline, hard work, and respect for learning that made it possible for her to get a law degree in the first place? Are we willing to conclude that, if the children of the welfare mother learn and practice such values, they won't be able to succeed because of their mother's income status?[20] The lives of such opposite black personalities as Jesse Jackson and Clarence Thomas nonetheless agree in suggesting that we would be wrong to do so.[21]

Because of its purportedly empirical character, modern social science abstracts from the moral elements involved in human behavior in favor of things that can be quantified more easily. We can measure a person's income. It's much harder to measure his or her self-discipline. We can base charts on who has which occupational title. It's much harder to measure the love of learning, the devotion to duty, the willingness to sacrifice immediate gratification in order to serve or realize a higher good. Moral decency is hard to quantify.

Ironically, this was precisely the reason black Americans facing unjust discrimination and repression developed a system of values based on moral, rather than material, things. In effect, they secured themselves against the depredations of a system devised to destroy their self-respect by storing their sense of personal worth in a form that made it hard to damage and hard to steal away. This was the secret of the enormous inner dignity that so many of us saw in our parents and grandparents, even though they did stoop labor, or worked as cooks, maids, porters, or launderers. Empirical social-science analyses can't easily measure such dignity. They find it hard to portray the little light that shines even in lowly hearts, the little light that was the great and secret strength of black survival in America.

An inwardly rooted sense of your own dignity is an important ingredient in the desire for self-improvement. It leads to the conviction that you're better than your circumstances, which in turn impels you to do something that will change those circumstances. The fact that black Americans developed a moral system that supported such an inner sense of dignity also meant that, despite all the pressure we faced to the contrary, we never abandoned the idea of self-improvement. The image of Pullman-car porters who could read Greek and Latin may seem incongruous, but it suggests a moral spirit that had already transcended the limits racial discrimination imposed. It suggests that, despite economic and social repression, it's possible to feel and respect in yourself the potential you are not allowed to realize.

This is what so many of our forebears had, and what so many of our offspring are losing or have lost. This is what comes of a strong sense of family, a deep capacity for religious faith, a hidden but unsinkable will to overcome. It's time we took a hard look at the unquantifiable essence that several decades of pseudosocial engineering appears almost to have destroyed. Before it's too late, we must make an attempt to recapture the sense of our own character that has almost slipped away. For we were poor, but we were rich in spirit; and though enslaved, we could be free in heart. We were kept in ignorance, but we fashioned from our experience the wisdom we needed to keep on marching toward the promised land. Those of our people who live in darkness today need to be reminded that a light shines within them, and that they, of all peoples, have the strength in their heritage to keep it alight.

This little light of mine, I'm gonna let it shine,
This little light of mine, I'm gonna let it shine,
This little light of mine, I'm gonna let it shine,
Let it shine, let it shine, let it shine.

Chapter 2

ALL

IN THE

FAMILY

From the early history of ancient Rome comes the story of a young Roman, Gaius Mucius, who was taken prisoner while attempting to assassinate a king whose army was besieging the city. The king condemned him to be burned alive, "whereupon Mucius, crying: 'See how cheap men hold their bodies when they care only for honour!' thrust his hand into the fire which had been kindled for sacrifice, and let it burn there as if he were unconscious of the pain."[1] From the power of such examples flowed the character of the all conquering Roman people. Of course, it's impossible to know how many young Romans living at the time had the same courage.[2] Mucius was probably atypical. But generally speaking, down through the ages, people have judged their ethnic stock more by its flowering genius than by its mundane roots and branches. Where ethnic character is concerned, they willingly subscribe to the doctrine that the exception proves the rule, so long as it's the right exception. The Italians have Caesar, Dante, and da Vinci; the French, Descartes, Napoleon, and de Gaulle; the British, Churchill, Wellington, and Isaac Newton. The people of Mongolia have lived in historic obscurity for several centuries, but they still see all their character epitomized in Genghis Khan. And so it goes. We live in the valleys of history, but our pride dwells upon its peaks.

Unfortunately, for black Americans, one of the subtle legacies of racial slavery is the American tendency to pervert this logic where we are concerned. Blacks who are exceptional in some positive sense are regarded as different from what is essentially black, rather than as proof of an intrinsic black potential.[3] Even among ourselves, there has been a tendency to look upon successful blacks as if they have somehow graduated from the community and no longer form a part of its meaning and definition.

On the other hand, the idea that the exception proves the rule has been systematically applied to negative facts about the black community, from slavery times until the present. E. Franklin Frazier points out that some enslavers, seeing how stoically some enslaved black mothers accepted the suffering or death of their children, concluded that "the master's feelings are sometimes even deeper than the mother's." As Frazier noted, "tradition has represented her as a devoted foster-parent to the master's children and indifferent to her own." Black fathers fared even more poorly. "According to the slaveholders, slave men had little sense of responsibility toward their families and abused them so mercilessly that Ole Massa constantly had to intervene to protect the women and children."[4] Influenced by the enslavers, the traditional and generally accepted view held that slavery emasculated black men by preventing them from providing for or defending their wives and children.

Yet, as more recent revisionist historians have amply documented, the evidence is overwhelming that enslaved blacks developed deep and lasting family bonds, stronger in many cases than the bonds of slavery. Genovese, for instance, cites the example of how "a slave in Virginia chopped his left hand off with a hatchet to prevent being sold away from his son." This enslaved man obviously loved and valued his son and family as much as the young

Roman Gaius Mucius loved the honor of his city. For such examples, Roman virtue was celebrated. Despite their similar heroism, black Americans were stigmatized as a people in whom the most basic human instincts had been crushed out.

In the 1960s, this traditional view gained currency and notoriety because of its role in arguments contained in the Moynihan report, released in 1965.[5,6] At the time, single-parent, female-headed households accounted for about a fifth of all black families. Single mothers accounted for nearly 25 percent of all black births. In the context of the received wisdom regarding slavery's effect on the black family,[7] Moynihan used such empirical data as evidence that the black family deviated from the American social norm "which presumes male leadership in private and public affairs." It was therefore pathologically defective.[8]

In and of itself, this conclusion displays and confirms the tendency toward a negative bias when dealing with facts about blacks. For the sake of the argument, let's assume for a moment that the traditional view is correct: Slavery not only intended to destroy but did destroy the basis for stable family life in the black community. This would mean that when slavery ended, blacks had no working concept of family life. If, one hundred years later, in the 1960s, we found that 80 percent of black children lived in families that corresponded to the norm, was that evidence of pathology, or of a remarkable recovery from the devastation wrought by the slave system? As we consider what implications it had for public policy, did it make sense to concentrate on the supposed weakness illustrated by the 20 percent, or the strengths suggested by the 80 percent? Even given the faulty historical premises he operated from, Moynihan could very reasonably (indeed, more reasonably) have reached different conclusions. Unhappily, in their thirst for influence over policy, many social scientists tend to accentuate the negative. Given traditional prejudices, the black community has been especially vulnerable to this tendency.

Nicholas Lemann has described the Moynihan report as "probably the most refuted document in American history (though of course its dire predictions about the poor black family all came true)."[9] Given the importance social scientists ascribe to predictive power, we have to suspect a little irony in this remark. But the report's critics saw ample reason to declare victory when Moynihan published another work, *Family and Nation*, in 1985. One of those critics, Andrew Billingsley, writes, with obvious satisfaction that "just twenty short years after his initial report, Daniel Moynihan said that what he thought was a peculiarly black family problem in 1965 'has now become the general condition.'" Billingsley argues that "large-scale technological and social forces increasingly impact on even more powerful and favored people" so that

> they too are beginning to show the same deviations from tra-
> ditional forms of family life as African-American families are.
> Some conspicuous examples of the changes are mothers in
> the work force, single-parent families, high divorce rates, teen
> pregnancy, and substance abuse. While these conditions are
> more prevalent among black families, they may no longer be
> considered uniquely black or as emanating from within
> African-American culture.[10]

Billingsley's sad joy at the general erosion of family life in America echoes the hopeful predictions made by some when the Moynihan report first came out.

> Joyce Ladner, a SNCC [Student Nonviolent Coordinating
> Committee] veteran who had joined the faculty at Howard,
> wrote in *tomorrow's tomorrow*, "Conceivably there will be no
> 'illegitimate' children and 'promiscuous' women in ten years
> if there are enough middle-class white women who decide
> they are going to disavow the societal canons regarding child-
> birth and premarital sexual behavior."[11]

As Ladner's attitude suggests, though, the fact that the general society has begun to show the same weakness as the black community doesn't necessarily refute the notion that this weakness arises from "a tangle of pathology" afflicting the black family. It may simply mean that the pathology has spread to the larger community. When some less-than-well-intentioned conservative spokesmen use the same breath to decry the collapse of family values and the rise of the welfare mentality, isn't this what they imply? We can't deal with the implication by rejoicing in the general breakdown of traditional morals, while tacitly accepting the assumption, implied in Moynihan's original argument, that family life in the black community never reflected those values.

This is the lie that needed to be and has been refuted.[12] Many in the liberal black elite are not at all anxious to admit this, however. As Ladner's remarks suggest, they wish to portray the black community as the natural ally of hard-line gays, feminists, and other ultraliberal social activists who seek to overthrow traditional norms. This can lead to some rather tortured and unconvincing presentations. Consider, for example, Billingsley's account of the black family structure.

> For the hundred-year period between the end of slavery and the aftermath of World War II the structure of African-American family life was characterized by a remarkable degree of stability. Specifically, the core of the traditional African-American family system has been the nuclear family composed of husband and wife and their own children. . . . As late as 1960 when uneducated black men could still hold good-paying blue-collar jobs in the industrial sector, 78 percent of all black families with children were headed by married couples. By 1970 only 64 percent of African-American families with children were headed by married couples. This declined steadily to a minority of 48 percent by 1980; and to 39 percent by 1990.[13]

Billingsley goes on to list and briefly discuss a variety of "alternative family structures": single-person households; cohabitation (opposite sex and same-sex marriagelike relationships); children, no marriage; marriage, no children; marriage and children; children and grandparents; blended families (with children from previous marriages); dual-earner families; commuter-couple families and augmented families ("units where nonrelatives live with the nuclear or extended family core"). He then concludes:

> The traditional two-parent, or simple, nuclear family which arose at the height of the industrial era has given way dramatically in relative terms to various alternative family structures. . . . Does this mean, as some suggest, that the African-American family is vanishing? Not at all. It means instead that families are doing what they always do. They are adapting as best they can to the pressures exerted upon them from their society in their gallant struggle to meet the physical, emotional, moral, and intellectual needs of their members.[14]

Given the fact that Billingsley himself alludes to the stability of the black family during the hundred years after slavery, it's impossible to understand how he justifies the conclusion that the black family is adapting the way it always has. The black household based on male-female marriage and cooperation had survived through the disappointments of Reconstruction, the era of Jim Crow persecution and disenfranchisement, and the decades of lynchings and legalized discrimination. But Billingsley finds nothing extraordinary in the notion that it should suddenly disintegrate because black men can no longer find "good-paying blue collar jobs in the industrial sector."

The notion that a significant number of blacks had access to *good-paying* blue-collar jobs is itself misleading. This is evident if one compares Billingsley's new argument with his discussion of the same facts in his earlier book (1968) on the black family. Billingsley's recent discussion (1992) presents figures on changes in the black working class that gloss over the essentially static situation in higher-income blue-collar categories prior to the 1940s.[15] He includes unskilled workers (to dramatize his point about the importance of the black working class), but neglects to point out what he noted in the previous work: "These are typically in the low-income occupations of unskilled and service workers. . . . It must be remarked that only about half of Negro workers can count on the kind of job status that provides economic security for their families." A chart in the earlier work shows that in 1910, only about 8 percent of all black workers had skilled or semiskilled blue-collar positions. By 1920, the figure rose to nearly 10 percent. During the 1920s and 1930s, it held steady at 12–13 percent. Dramatic increases did not occur until the forties, so that by 1950, this category had jumped to about 24 percent of the black workforce. In 1960, it was at 26 percent, and in 1965, 40 percent.[16] Unfortunately for Billingsley's theory about the black family, this category held steady through the mid 1970s,[17] yet the decline in black two-parent families with children was well under way by 1970. Billingsley emphatically declares: "The decline in the black working class since 1960 has been the single most important force responsible for the decline in the nuclear-family structure over this period."[18] Given the facts, however, we can accept this assertion only if we are willing to believe that the effect preceded the cause.[19]

In any case, as Billingsley previously admitted, working-class status did not mean economic security for families. Why should the decline in working-class status (part of which is due to the rapid expansion of the black middle class) lead to family disintegration? Consider, moreover, the facts Herbert Gutman presents with regard to the black community in New York City in 1905. He compares it with the Italian and Jewish communities of the same era.

Most Jewish (73 percent) and Italian (86 percent) men studied were blue-collar wage earners in 1905. So were most
blacks (95 percent). But this similarity hid very important
differences between the black workers and the Jewish and
Italian workers, differences similar to those that had distinguished southern urban blacks from white southern urban
workers and from the 1880 Paterson native white and Irish
workers. Nearly three of five Jewish male *workers* (59 percent)
had skills, and nearly one of two (45 percent) Italian male
workers had skills, but less than one of ten black *workers* (9
percent) had skills. . . . The Jews and Italians experienced far
greater occupational diversity than the blacks. . . . It was
much, much more difficult to be black and lower class than
to be white and lower class in New York City in 1905.[20]

What is remarkable, though, is that 80 percent of black households
were "kin related with a nuclear core," compared with 96 and 95
percent respectively for Jews and Italians.[21] The economic disparity
between blacks and the others emphatically did not lead to a correspondingly wide disparity in family structure. For blacks, blue-
collar jobs didn't mean economic security, but economic hardship
didn't lead to the collapse of the black community's moral
infrastructure.

In 1965, Moynihan insisted that slavery crushed the black-
American family while staring at clear proof that, at the time, some
80 percent of the community's families had defied their intended
fate. Billingsley cites the successful hundred-year record of that
defiance, then argues incoherently that blue-collar unemployment
doomed the traditional black family structure. Both ignore the possibility that the black family structure reflects the choices that
black Americans made in the past and that, for better or worse,
they are making today.

We can best approach this possibility by considering in greater
detail the situation black Americans faced during the slavery period.

The marriages of enslaved people had no legal status. Their families were subject to arbitrary dissolution when family members were sold or carried away by enslavers. These families had, as such, no economic base. Billingsley puts it succinctly: "In short, there was the absence, in the United States, of societal support and protection for the Negro family as a physical, social or economic unit."[22]

It might be more accurate to say that no consistent protection or support existed. Some enslavers thought family bonds made enslaved blacks better workers and contributed to more orderly behavior. Religious and moral scruples led others to encourage marriage among the enslaved. White churches and ministers sometimes exerted a positive influence in this regard. In *The Slave Community*, John Blassingame writes: "Abolition doubts notwithstanding, thousands of slaves were married in Southern churches between 1800 and 1860. . . . At many times between 1830 and 1860 more slaves were married in the Episcopal churches in some states than were whites."

None of these motives, however, prevented enslavers from breaking black families apart. In one account: "I seen chillun sold off and de mammy not sold, and sometimes de mammy sold and a little baby kept on de place and give to another woman to raise. Dem white folks didn't care nothing 'bout how de slaves grieved when dey tore up a family."[23] In another report:

> In spite of the fact that probably a majority of the planters tried to prevent family separations in order to maintain plantation discipline, practically all of the black autobiographers were touched by the tragedy. Death occurred too frequently in the master's house, creditors were too relentless in collecting their debts, the planter's reserves ran out too often, and the master longed too much for expensive items for the slave to escape the clutches of the slave trader. Nothing demonstrated his powerlessness as much as the slave's inability to prevent the forcible sale of his wife and children.[24]

Genovese says that some enslavers went to great pains to keep families together.[25] Gutman criticizes Genovese because his work lacks a "sustained analysis of how local and interregional sale, involuntary migration with an owner, gift transfer, and estate division affected the immediate slave family and enlarged slave kin group." Gutman concludes that "the best available evidence . . . discloses that about one in six (or seven) slave marriages were ended by force or sale . . ."[26] Whatever the exact incidence, the ever-present possibility of such separations represented a "painful uncertainty which in one form or another was ever obtruding itself in the pathway of the slave."[27] Blassingame describes this as "a haunting fear which made all of the slave's days miserable." He feelingly sums up the emotional trauma:

> To be sold away from his relatives or stand by and see a mother, a sister, a brother, a wife, or a child turn away from him was easily the most traumatic event of his life. Strong men pleaded, with tears in their eyes, for their master to spare their loved ones. Mothers screamed and clung grimly to their children only to be kicked away by the slave trader. Others lost their heads and ran off with their children or vainly tried to fight off overseer, master and slave trader. Angry, despondent and overcome by grief, the slaves frequently never recovered from the shock of separation.[28]

The grief enslaved blacks felt on being separated from their families offered historians an important clue to the deep emotional importance of their family ties. E. Franklin Frazier's work on the black family left unchallenged many of the negative stereotypes of enslaved people. But even he acknowledged the significance of this grief:

> The devotion of mothers to their own children was often demonstrated in their sacrifices to see them when they were sep-

arated from them. . . . slave mothers, instead of viewing with indifference the sale, or loss otherwise, of their children, often put up stubborn resistance and suffered cruel punishments to prevent separation from them.[29]

One consequence of this trauma was that family break-ups were an important motive for escape attempts. "Almost every study of runaway slaves uncovers the importance of the family motive. . . . Next to resentment over punishment, the attempt to find relatives was the most prevalent cause of flight."[30]

As a general rule, though, family attachments were a weighty reason for resisting the temptation to run. Frederick Douglass said that "thousands would escape from slavery . . . but for the strong cords of affection that bind them to their family, relatives, and friends." Another escapee wrote: "It required all the moral courage I was master of to suppress my feelings while taking leave of my little family."[31] In fact, the desire to be near a spouse led some freed blacks to live as though still in bondage:

My paw's name was Tom Vaughn. . . . He saw my maw on the Kilpatrick place and her man was dead. He told Dr. Kilpatrick, my massa, he'd buy my maw and her three chillun with all the money he had, iffen he'd sell her. But Dr. Kilpatrick was never one to sell any but the old niggers who was only part workin' in the fields and past their breedin' times. So my paw marries my maw and works the fields, same as any other nigger.[32]

Though the slave system greatly complicated and detracted from their ability to fulfill parental roles, the enslaved strove constantly to be true fathers and mothers. Within the severe limits of their servitude, they sought to nurture and provide for their offspring. They also tried to pass on the manners and morals their children needed to physically survive and mentally endure captivity. The lessons weren't always easy for pride to swallow.

> One of the most important lessons for the child was learning to hold his tongue around white folks. This was especially true on those plantations where masters tried to get children to spy on their parents. . . . Learning to accept personal abuse and the punishment of loved ones passively was one of the most difficult lessons for the slave child.[33]

Side by side with such survival skills, however, parents, by word and example, inculcated a sense of personal pride that put limits on the insults and indignities enslaved blacks would endure. Enslavers knew full well that excesses could and did give rise to fierce reactions, as men lashed out against the violators of mothers, wives, sisters, and sweethearts, or women rose up in defense of their siblings and their young.

In his study of records relating to the years during and immediately after the Civil War, the historian Herbert Gutman saw "the powerful expression of affective Afro-American familial and kin beliefs and behavior . . ." *The Black Family in Slavery and Freedom* explores and amply substantiates the strength of the family as a moral idea among the enslaved, and leaves little doubt that "large numbers of slave couples lived in long marriages and most slaves lived in double-headed households." Though childbirth before marriage was common (as it is in some parts of Africa), this did not involve the abandonment of the quest for stable, two-parent, family cores. In addition, the enslaved blacks remained conscious of their participation in an extended family network, a consciousness expressed and maintained in their naming practices. Gutman also describes persuasively "how and why slave kin obligation was transformed into an enlarged slave conception of social obligations which, in turn, served as the underlying social basis of developing slave communities."[34]

Yet, in view of the universally admitted hostility of the slavery system to black marriages, and the absence of any reliable external supports for them, we would expect to find that enslaved blacks didn't form or remain in stable marriage relationships. Marriage is intrinsically a social institution. Societal support, in law and custom, is what distinguishes marriage from other, more fortuitous, sexual relationships. The need for elaborate social support is a reflection upon human nature. Apparently, it requires a lot of effort to maintain stable, monogamous relationships between men and women. There seems to be no guarantee that, left to the promptings of their unadorned animal nature, men and women would naturally end up establishing such relationships. This is probably why the laws and customs regulating marriage have absorbed so much attention and energy in civilized societies throughout human experience. Until our own times, this went beyond passive social support. Most societies strongly encouraged, indeed practically compelled, people to marry, especially if there was any evidence that they were already "in the family way."

Yet, though the slave system did not encourage strong black families, a large number of enslaved blacks tried to maintain them anyway. For many, this was a simple act of moral will through which, regardless of their circumstances, they asserted their humanity. No one demanded that they care about their kin; they simply did. Moreover, even though this caring entailed physical pain and danger, as well as enormous emotional distress, they would not let it go. As E. Franklin Frazier concluded: "It is not surprising that [Negro] family life without the support of custom and a venerated tradition, has tended towards instability, but rather that it has shown such vitality."[35]

It's not enough, however, for us to make note of this fact, praise our enslaved ancestors for their will and courage, and go on. We need to consider what their actions tell us about the moral ideas of marriage and the family that motivated them. Today, many people tend to look at these institutions strictly in terms of the individual satisfaction that people derive from them. The assumption is that people can't or won't remain in a relationship if the pain and suffering they derive from it too greatly exceeds the satisfaction it gives them. So divorce becomes commonplace, extending now even to the possibility that children can "divorce" their parents. Today, it seems almost shocking and offensive to suggest that people should sacrifice themselves for the sake of their children, or in order to show respect for the idea of marriage or the family.

Yet it's very hard to believe that the risk-laden personal gratification family ties afforded enslaved blacks simply outweighed the fear and grief they could expect to suffer if they clung fast to their family relationships. What's more likely is that they knew that grief, danger, and disappointment were unavoidable and that to keep family feeling alive would entail great sacrifice. They did not hold on to the idea of family out of any assured expectation of personal self-fulfillment. For them, it involved instead the prospect of personal suffering and sacrifice. But they kept it alive.

Why? Herbert Gutman acknowledges that this is the question that he and the colleagues who reviewed his work inevitably raised. The answer is undoubtedly as complex as were the enslaved people themselves, yet one word suggests itself again and again as we read the accounts and analyses of their behavior. That word is *faith*— what Webster describes as "firm belief in something for which there is no proof." It also means *loyalty* and *trust*. The slave system generally conspired, for instance, to deny black men the marks of manhood. This began in childhood when "boys, like girls, wore dresses until the age of about twelve or when they went to the fields."[36] As grown-ups, the enslaved men were hard put to provide for or defend their families, and they were even more likely than women to be separated from their children. Enslavers generally marked descent through the female, so even the man's biological role received scant formal recognition. Yet "the slaves rarely named daughters for their mothers and regularly named sons for their fathers . . . dramatically affirming the important cultural role of the slave father. . . ."[37]

Enslaved people also named children for grandparents, aunts, and uncles as well, thereby sketching out the network of kinship support children could count on as they grew. It was an act of faith, often faithfully rewarded. Enslaved family members hid runaways, and those who were free worked for years to purchase ones still enslaved.

Peter Randolph's brother, for instance, ran away and stayed in the woods seven months while his mother carried him food. Sold South, William Grimes's sister returned to be near her husband, hid in the woods for years, and bore three children there.[38]

In 1839, a Frenchman purchased Milton Clarke's sister Delia, freed and married her, and took her to New Orleans. Years later, Clarke hired out as a steamboat worker and searched several times in New Orleans before finding her. She then returned to Kentucky to visit her family and planned to raise money to purchase her two brothers.[39]

One man's uncles worked together and "bought themselves three times," eventually buying freedom for their sister and nephew as well. They persevered despite being "cheated out of their freedom in the first instance."[40] It was an act of faith.

Such as it is, the historical record of the era of captivity offers many such instances. Who knows what others have been lost to memory. Yet in a way, they simply confirm what common sense might suggest, if our national prejudices didn't get in the way. The enslaved lived in a world that formally and in many ways materially denied their essential humanity. Yet in the shadow of the valley of death, they sang, they prayed, they loved, and laughed and wept just as if they knew it wasn't so. In the world manufactured by their oppressors, the evidence was all against them and the verdict prearranged, but still, they insisted on living as if justice would some day be done. In this sense, their whole lives and existence was an act of faith, which their circumstances tested and continually betrayed, but which they never surrendered.

Didn't my Lord deliver Daniel, deliver Daniel, deliver Daniel,
Didn't my Lord deliver Daniel, and why not every man?
He delivered Daniel from the lion's den
And Jonah from the belly of the whale
And the Hebrew children from the fiery furnace,
Why not deliver poor me?

Chapter 3

THE LITTLE

WHEEL

RUN BY

FAITH

D espite all the sacrifice involved, black Americans held on to the idea of family. Despite consistent and sometimes brutal obstacles and disappointments, they continued to strive in the belief that something better was possible. They did all this because they were a people of faith. At the communal level, the black church embodied this faith. For a long time it was the central, indeed the only, expression of the community's existence. This may be the most important clue to black-American identity, more important than skin color or African roots. It means that, as defined by our own experience, black-American identity is a matter of moral and religious conviction. Like that of the Old Testament Israelites, the identity of black Americans as a people has emerged as a consequence of our struggle to define and hold fast to some principle of good that we can believe in and live by, in spite of all the evil we have endured.

As it is still too often written, we are encouraged to conceive of history as a series of decisive moments that shape human destiny. In fact, such moments take shape over time through the lives and actions of the multitudes of people who remain invisible and anonymous beneath the surface of great events. The same faith that could inspire militancy fueled perseverance, as the enslaved faced the challenges of everyday life under slavery. It nourished the determination to sustain family ties, despite all the burdens slavery placed upon them. It supported the enslaved's ability to retain a decent respect for the ideal of marriage-based sexual relations, even when the depravity of the slave system led to practices that fell far short of the ideal. Herbert Gutman reports on the apparent pattern of child-bearing that often prevailed among black women, during and in the aftermath of slavery. Premarital sexual relations, including several out-of-wedlock births, were not unusual. Yet frequently, the same women would end up in stable marriages that lasted forty or fifty years. Moral absolutism in sexual matters was hardly sustainable among people who had been subject to the harsh vagaries of life in bondage. Yet, as we have seen, the moral confusion slavery involved did not unavoidably destroy the black American's moral sensibility. Here, the Christian doctrine of repentance, forgiveness, and rebirth played an important role. Through their discovery or rediscovery of Christian faith, men and women who strayed at one stage of their lives could signify their decision to live according to conventional moral ideals and standards. Christian concepts and rituals offered individuals the means to reclaim moral sovereignty over their own lives, in a context that allowed them to receive, then eventually add their weight to, the moral resources of the black community. In this way, Christian faith helped to keep the marriage-based family resilient despite the high incidence of sexual activity outside of marriage. Four authors address this point:

White churches continued to exercise moral oversight over the slaves after their weddings. Frequently investigating charges of adultery and fornication, the churches tried to promote the development of Christian moral precepts in the quarters. Consequently, they often excommunicated or publicly criticized slaves for abandoning their mates, having pre-marital pregnancies, and engaging in extramarital sex. . . . An overwhelming majority of the cases were brought to the attention of the church by the slave members . . .[1]

African churches strengthened the black family by insisting that marriages be solemnized by religious services, punishing adulterers, and occasionally reuniting separated couples.[2]

The churches became . . . the most important agency of social control among Negroes. The churches undertook as organizations to censure unconventional and immoral sex behavior and to punish by expulsion sex offenders and those who violated the monogamous mores.[3]

After the Civil War, the Black churches legitimized the informal marriages of many former slaves, demanded marital fidelity, designed programs to foster male leadership in the family, encouraged honest hard work, affirmed individual self-worth, and urged the family to function as an "extended church" by conducting family worship within the home.[4]

The black church's role took firm root, as we see from E. Franklin Frazier's discussion of illegitimacy among rural black women in the 1930s.

Our account, so far, of illegitimacy in the rural communities in the South would seem to indicate that neither the families of the women nor the community express any moral disapproval of this type of behavior. That this is not universally true is suggested by the remark of the wife in a family that included two of her children before marriage as well as two of her husband's since marriage. She explained, concerning her illegitimate children, that she had had them before becoming a member of the church. The community expresses its disapproval of moral delinquencies almost exclusively through the church. We have previously noted cases in which women have been turned out of the church because they gave birth to illegitimate children.[5]

Christianity helped oppressed blacks maintain a sense of their own worth and dignity. It helped them to sustain the moral ideal of the family. It also helped them to achieve and act upon an idea of community independent of the individuals and powers that oppressed them. In the context of slavery, this was an extraordinarily difficult achievement. The ideology of slavery denigrated black social instincts and impulses. It encouraged the myth that the enslavers cared more for their captives than they did for one another. In fact, enslavers fostered divisions between field slaves and house slaves, between drivers and common laborers. Enslaved people were used to whip one another, they were encouraged to spy and inform on one another. All in all, everything was done to make blacks' fear of or attachment to the enslavers, and indeed to whites generally, more powerful than their capacity to love or trust one another. Here again, though, the concepts of Christian doctrine mingled with lingering resonances of African communalism to work against the influences of the slave system. As black Christianity allowed individuals to assert their moral responsibility for themselves, so black congregations and churches gave institutional expression to the caring concern blacks felt toward one another, and ultimately, the obligation they felt toward the black community as such.

To some extent, the black church began to emerge even in the midst of slavery. With practices that frequently combined Christian elements with remnants and cadences of African tradition, enslaved people gave comfort and support to one another in times of sickness, and in the face of death. In one report, slaves "helped each other in illness as in death. If a woman fell ill, 'other women came over to help her with the chillen, or to cook the meals, wash the clothes or to do other necessary chores.' "6 In another account:

> A slave funeral became a pageant, a major event, a community effort at once solemn and spirited. The slaves preferred to have a service, but they would not readily do without a display. In this way, they carried on West African tradition, according to which a proper funeral would put the departed spirit to rest and would guarantee against the return of a stirring ghost—a view held by some rural southern blacks during the twentieth century.[7]

As is generally the case in human societies, the care the enslaved bestowed on funeral rites said more about their concept of life than death. The funeral not only brought the community together physically, it represented the continuity between generations, the thread of love and respect that bound past, present, and future generations. The burial ritual was one of the only displays of unalloyed self-respect the enslaved enjoyed, an outward display of what their religious faith inwardly affirmed.

In the context of these communal displays black preachers came forth, among blacks enslaved as well as free. "Drivers, artisans, and ordinary field slaves of special force of personality turned to preaching. Precisely those slaves and free Negroes who had the strength to lead their fellows took up the Word."[8] Since enslaved black preachers operated within the constraints of the slave system, they were not free to say and do whatever they pleased. They could not openly preach rebellion, and indeed, usually had to repeat the exhortations to obedience and respect for the enslavers that the slave system demanded as the price of religious expression.[9] But as Herskovits points out, "Whatever the attention given to 'religious instruction'[10] of the slaves in various areas and at various periods of slavery, the freedom of the slaves to conduct their own services without white supervision was always greater than their freedom to work or organize politically in the African manner."[11]

> On the plantations and farms the slaves met for services apart from the whites whenever they could. Weekly services on Sunday evenings were common. . . . The slaves' religious meetings would be held in secret when their masters forbade all such; or when their masters forbade all except Sunday meetings; or when rumors of rebellion or disaffection led even indulgent masters to forbid them so as to protect the people from trigger-happy patrollers; or when the slaves wanted to make sure that no white would hear them. Only during in-surrection scares or tense moments occasioned by political turmoil could the law against such meetings be enforced.[12]

Where permitted, religious meetings were the only serious pub-lic gatherings available to the enslaved. They could provide an op-portunity for black people to assemble on a regular basis in a context not entirely dominated by the enslaver. Naturally, the en-slaved preacher became a focus of communal consciousness:

> He was able to unify the blacks, console the sick, weak, and fearful, uplift and inspire them. Suffering with his flock, he understood their tribulations and was accepted as a coun-selor and arbiter in the quarters. In his sermons the slaves often saw the invisible hand of God working for their earthly freedom and retribution against the whites. Whatever the content of the sermons, the slaves preferred a black preacher.[13]

White prejudices combined with black preferences to produce sep-arate black congregations. But in the context of slavery, these con-gregations could by no means become truly independent churches.

The recognition which the whites accorded to the Negro "congregations" was accorded them as segments of the white organizations. White control of these segments was never completely relaxed. Therefore, there was always some tension because the slaves preferred their own preachers and wanted to conduct their religious services according to their own mode of worshipping. . . . The tension was never resolved and the Negro church never emerged as an independent institution except under the Negroes who were free before the Civil War.[14]

It was among free blacks, therefore, that black churches first appeared as independent community institutions.[15] The black churches established by free blacks before the Civil War became the model and often the organizational root of the independent churches that proliferated among blacks once the slave system fell. They first emerged in the flush of egalitarianism and religious revival that followed the American Revolutionary War. The idealistic spirit of the Revolution led to some racially mixed congregations, especially in the evangelical denominations. It was not long, however, before white prejudices produced discrimination that insulted black pride and stimulated racial separatism.

The most famous of the Negro preachers in the North was . . . Richard Allen. . . . When Allen observed in Philadelphia the need of the Negroes for religious leadership and an organization, he proposed that a separate church be established for Negroes. His proposal was opposed by whites and Negroes. However, when the number of Negroes attending St. George Methodist Episcopal Church increased, Negroes were removed from the seats around the wall and ordered to sit in the gallery. Mistaking the section of the gallery which they were to occupy, Allen, Absalom Jones, and another member were almost dragged from their knees as they prayed. They left the church and together with other Negro members founded the Free African Society.[16]

Although it is unclear when various Methodist churches began to segregate Negroes, in the 1780s several Baltimore freemen withdrew from the Methodist meetinghouse in a dispute over seating arrangements.[17]

The Allen story illustrates the combination of positive preference and reaction against discrimination that motivated blacks to establish separate black churches. Especially in the South, this movement often met with strong white resistance. "Whites worried that independent, unsupervised black religion fostered all kinds of subversion."[18] The fact that African churches in Charleston were named by informers as centers for the insurrectionary Vesey conspiracy in South Carolina reinforced such worries. They eventually gave way, however, to black pressure and a view among whites that combined paternalism with the belief that the encouragement of religion would make blacks easier to control. By the 1850s, black churches existed throughout the South, particularly in urban areas.

Wherever they were established, African churches quickly became the centers of black religious life. In spite of watchful white supervisors and meddling white trustees, blacks flocked to the new churches. . . . Although precise figures are not available, it is probable that a higher percentage of Negroes than whites were regular churchgoers.[19]

Throughout the South, black life revolved around the church. Many freemen were baptized, married, and buried in the same church. . . . The church was more than a source of discipline; it was a center for education, a provider of social insurance, and a place where blacks might relax and organize community entertainment. African churches supported schools and fraternal associations; church choirs gave concerts; church auxiliaries sponsored fairs, picnics, and banquets. The church expressed the community's social conscience by aiding the poor, supporting missionary activities, and helping other free Negro communities establish like institutions.[20]

The black church has never surrendered its central position in the lives and hearts of the black multitudes. Yet black elites and intellectuals have always been reluctant to acknowledge this fact, and have never seen it as cause for celebration. In *Black Culture and Black Consciousness*, Lawrence Levine argues that religious faith was central to black culture before the Civil War, but lost that central position thereafter. V. P. Franklin disputes Levine's contention that the religious worldview was central in the culture of the enslaved. He concludes that "the shared experience of racial oppression occupied the central position in defining the emerging value system of the Afro-American masses."[21] Both Levine and Franklin, however, base their conclusions on the existence or absence of a secular folk culture. This begs the question. The existence of secular songs and stories does not of necessity mean that secular values have displaced religious ones. A better indication of the importance of the religious view might be evidence of church participation and attendance, which has been uniformly high among blacks in the post-slavery period.[22] In fact, for all the talk of powerful secular movements among black Americans, no secular effort, including Garvey's Universal Negro Improvement Association (UNIA),[23] has ever come close to the combined millions participating in black churches. In fact, most of the secular organizations within the black community, including those in the economic sector, took root from within the black church.

The Black Church has no challenger as the cultural womb of the black community. Not only did it give birth to new institutions such as schools, banks, insurance companies, and low-income housing, it also provided an academy and an arena for political activities, and it nurtured young talent for musical, dramatic, and artistic development.[24]

For all the talk among elite black intellectuals about the black masses, they have been consistently unwilling to acknowledge the primacy of the one truly mass-based institution in the black community. E. Franklin Frazier undoubtedly spoke for many elite intellectuals when he wrote that "the Negro church and Negro religion have cast a shadow over the entire intellectual life of Negroes and have been responsible for the so-called backwardness of American Negroes."[25]

The black church has long had to labor against the argument that black Christianity is derivative, something borrowed from, or imposed by, the dominant European culture after enslavement ripped blacks from their authentic African religious roots. This argument reflects the habit of looking at blacks as a people whose identity is entirely conditioned by external forces—slavery, poverty, racism. It ignores the possibility that, however great the external forces acting upon them, black Americans retained a capacity for moral self-determination. This willful denial of our human potential once again reflects the heritage of slavery, the habit of looking at black-American history solely from the perspective of the enslavers. If we accept the definition of the slave system, then the enslaved could have nothing that was truly their own. Seeing blacks in this way, it's natural to conclude that their Christianity was simply imposed upon them by the enslavers. Yet the historians of slavery agree that enslavers had no uniform view on the advisability of Christianizing the enslaved population. Some enslavers encouraged it, others did not. Some saw it as a means of pacification and control, others feared the destabilizing effects of the doctrine of moral equality Christianity entails. Admitting blacks into the Christian fold directly contradicted the assumption that they were chattel no different from cattle or horses. Mere beasts of burden make unfit candidates for baptism. Furthermore, some white Christians held the converse to be true as well; that is, fit candidates for baptism should not be treated like beasts. From this they drew the conclusion that baptism logically implied emancipation. Among enslavers who feared this logic, some openly resisted Christianization.

Even if enslavers had held a uniformly encouraging view of Christian conversion, this would not have precluded a moral preference on the part of the enslaved. In fact, the enslaver view was nonuniform and to a degree self-contradictory.[26] This left their captives ample room for reflection and choice. Further evidence of this lies in the fact that not all enslaved people adopted or practiced Christianity even where it was available.

Finally, we should consider the nature of Christianity itself. Christianity is a religion of conscience. Mere conformity to rituals and rules leads to the "whited sepulcher" practitioners that Christ explicitly condemns. Beyond this general characteristic, enslaved people frequently had a choice of denominations. They most often gravitated toward the churches that placed great emphasis on the demonstrative personal and emotional bond between Christ and the believer, as opposed to the more formal and intellectual bases of faith that characterized high church Protestantism and Catholicism. This means that enslaved people preferred the Christian sects that required an intense, personal commitment, the sects in which one's expression of faith could not be dictated or predetermined by the outside authority of the enslavers or anyone else.

The Christianity that was spread among slaves during the First and Second Awakenings was an evangelical Christianity that stressed personal conversion through a deep regenerating experience, being "born again." The spiritual journey began with an acknowledgment of personal sinfulness and unworthiness and ended in an emotional experience of salvation by God through the Holy Spirit. The rebirth meant a change, a fundamental reorientation in the approach to life.[27]

The preference among black Americans for the Methodist and Freewill Baptist sects reflected something more than the conjuncture of their proselytizing zeal with the emotional side of the black personality. Frazier, with a hint of condescension, ascribes the preference essentially to black emotionalism:

> Negroes found in the fiery message of salvation a hope and a prospect of escape from their earthly woes. Moreover, the emphasis which the preachers placed upon feeling as a sign of conversion found a ready response in the slaves who were repressed in so many ways. . . . In the emotionalism of the camp meetings and revivals, some social solidarity, even if temporary, was achieved.[28]

Here, as too often in his work, Frazier observes accurately, but without accurately thinking through the significance of what he observes. As Genovese points out:

> Methodism, on the face of it, hardly seems a likely candidate for the affections of a high-spirited, life-loving people. Grim, humorless, breathing the fires of damnation—notwithstanding love feasts and some joyful hymns—it was more calculated to associate Jesus with discipline and order than with love.[29]

Methodism doesn't seem to offer much relief from emotional repression. But what Richard Allen called "the plain simple gospel" of the Methodists makes salvation, and therefore the dignity of hope, accessible even to the most lowly and powerless. Genovese later alludes to the fact that "predestinarian doctrine did not appear in black religion":

> The slave quarters provided poor ground for predestinarianism. When slaves and ex-slaves insisted that God had fore-

ordained everything, they usually meant that even slavery had an appropriate place in his eternal design. And at that, their reaction could turn bitter.[30]

Is it really surprising that enslaved people preferred a faith grounded in the possibility of human freedom? What, besides elitist prejudices, would lead one to ascribe such a reasonable (under the circumstances) preference to mere emotionalism? Blacks preferred these sects precisely because they gave greater scope and authority to the individual's inward experience. They postulated a direct relationship with the Supreme Being, the Supreme Power. By its very nature, this postulate set the stage for the psychological subversion of the slave system.

The enslaver culture itself contributed to this subversion. Even where the enslavers allowed or encouraged Christianization, Christian precepts were frequently honored in the breach. This meant, for instance, that most enslavers did not apply to their captives the Christian concept of permanent, lifelong marriages or strict sexual mores. When economic or other considerations required it, they dissolved marriages, broke up families, or encouraged sexual relations outside of marriage. In addition, of course, there was the overriding fact that to control the enslaved their captors imposed a harsh regime of violence in the service of worldly ends, a regime inherently at odds with the "turn the other cheek" doctrines of Christian peace and love. Within the enslaver culture, therefore, Christianity did not govern at the social level, nor often at the individual level. Blacks responding to the enslaver culture could not experience Christianity in its pure form. Instead, they encountered it in a socially subordinate, instrumental role. This gave them scope to construct their own unique brand of Christianity, one in which the basic concepts of right and justice, as well as the application of ethical precepts and discipline, reflected the thorny realities of their oppressed situation.[31] Rather than seeing religion as representing a strict external authority dictating behavior, enslaved people felt it to be an inner resource, an integral component of their moral and physical survival.

This more organic approach to religion was probably a consequence of the surviving spirit of the African religions enslaved blacks carried with them from Africa.[32] In principle, one major distinction between ancient paganism[33] and the Judeo-Christian or Islamic religions lies in the fact that, among the pagans, religion is regarded as an integral expression of the practical needs of the community and its members. It is part of the social reality formed by the relationships that make up the community—both human relations (e.g., common ancestors and the kinship relations derived from them), and the relations between humans and natural phenomena (the indwelling spirits of natural locales, objects, or forces). Religion does not form or reform the community, since it is the symbolic expression of its natural form. By contrast, both Judaism and Christianity are religions of reform. In both, religion is supposed to reform and structure the community to reflect man's relationship with a transcendent God. It is supposed to become the ethical basis of individual and communal life, not a symbolic expression of its physical or natural basis. In the Old Testament, this was the significance and practical effect of the forty years the Israelites spent wandering in the desert under God's tutelage. In the New Testament, Christ, through the charismatic influence of his example, achieves the same result, one individual at a time. His effect is predicated on the notion that once converted, the individual becomes the agent of his religious conviction. He becomes a member of the Church, a part of the body of Christ, owing his first allegiance there, not to the secular society in which he happens to exist.[34]

Since Christianity was fundamentally at odds with the principles of enslavement, in order to exist in a community based upon slavery, it had to give up this ethically dominant role. Thus, from the enslaved person's point of view, the evident inconsistencies between the enslaver's beliefs and practices undermined the moral authority of Christian whites.[35] Enslaved people felt no moral compulsion to respect or adopt the self-defeated Christianity of their temporal masters.[36]

> I have heard the mistress ring the bell for family prayer, and I have seen the servants immediately begin to sneer and laugh; and have heard them declare that they would not go in to prayers; adding, if I go in she will not only just read "Servants obey your master"; but she will not read "Break every yoke, and let the oppressed go free." I have seen colored men at the church door, scoffing *at the ministers*, while they were preaching and saying, "You had better go home, and set your slaves free."[37]

Moreover, since the slave system could without warning force them into behavior that contradicted strictly stated Christian principles (those regarding sexual relations outside of marriage, for instance), enslaved people had to pick their way through a moral minefield, using the spirit of Christian faith, rather than the letter of Christian law, as their guide. Thus the realm of religion and morality necessarily represented an area of personal autonomy, an escape route to inner freedom kept open by the moral contradictions of enslaver society.

> As long as the slaves remained faithful to God's will, they would be saved. But this was far from easy, especially in situations where the slaveholders would not allow regular religious services among the slaves. In those instances, the slaves would have to sneak off to their "prayer grounds" and "brush arbors" to praise God and pray for their deliverance. . . . In teaching the enslaved Afro-Americans to ignore or disobey the rules of the slaveholders and praise God among themselves, slave religion fostered self-determinist values. . . .[38]

In its supposedly most benign paternalistic form, the slave system regarded blacks as children. They were to be treated humanely, but never freed from the authority and discipline of the master race. But here, too, Christianity subverted the falsely exculpatory metaphor of enslavement.[39] Christ spoke of all people as children of God. The key distinction among people in Christian doctrine is not between children and adults, but between those who, in their conduct, respect the innocence of childlike spirituality, and those who instead give occasion to scandal and corruption. Christ speaks of the childlike condition as the sine qua non of citizenship in the heavenly kingdom.[40] He reserves words of special opprobrium for those who offend against childlike believers. In Christian terms, therefore, the slave system's intended degradation of black humanity becomes an elevation of moral status for black believers, who can see themselves as true examples of the childlike faithful. By contrast, far from being morally superior beings on whom blacks must rely for discipline, enslavers appear as the worst kind of offenders, for whom God has reserved a particularly scorching spot in hell.

The central event of Christian theology, Christ's crucifixion and resurrection, had special resonance for the enslaved. Like the enslaved, Christ was unjustly held, unjustly beaten, unjustly forced to labor toward his own destruction, unjustly put to death. Yet his passion was the prelude to the ultimate triumph over evil. Black captives who sang, "Were you there when they crucified my Lord?" answered without hesitation, because for them, crucifixion was a daily event, the stuff that their lives were made of. This placed them in a special relationship with their Redeemer, in whose suffering they saw a clear precursor of their own. At the same time, Christ's Resurrection offered a cogent metaphor through which to reinterpret the pain and humiliation of slavery. Rather than extinguishing humanity as the slave system intended, the enslaved persons' Christlike tribulations could be seen as the prelude to spiritual redemption, through which their humanity might be preserved not just for now, but for eternity. Whether the captives' experience took on this redeeming quality depended on their own choices, their own actions, but most especially on their own faith.

According to the logic of slavery, the enslaved did not own herself. Her body could be abused in order to gratify the needs, whims, and lusts of her master.[41] For those enslaved people who believed that the physical body is the self, enslavement meant moral annihilation. The Christian faith, however, relies on a concept of the self that transcends the physical body. This concept makes it possible to believe that physical bondage cannot destroy the capacity for spiritual self-determination. Earthly masters may control the physical body, but God alone dispenses the grace that energizes the spiritual self. The Christian also believes that the spirit has priority, that faith can move mountains, that the physical, earthly powers are ultimately subject to the spiritual. Spiritual self-determination therefore implies the ability to break the physical chains that bind. The Christian believes that faithful prayer has the power to transform this world, a transformation that begins with the personal life and habits of the individual. Since charity and fellow feeling are such important parts of Christian ethics, however, this personal transformation is expressed in ways that affect and may transform others, until by this means, entire communities are renewed in the spirit of Christ.

Most contemporary historians acknowledge that Christianity offered enslaved blacks at least a psychological escape from the vicissitudes of life under slavery. Some also have suggested that religious gatherings, songs, and other expressions were part of the culture of physical resistance against slavery, figuring importantly in insurrections and escape efforts. On the negative side, however, elite intellectuals have criticized black Christianity on the grounds that its promise of joy and salvation in a life to come tended to defuse blacks' anger against the injustices they suffered in this world.[42] V. P. Franklin describes this as characteristic of "the predominant ideological positions about the nature and significance of

Afro-American religion in the first half of the twentieth century." He continues:

> Progressive radicals and Communists of the 1920s, such as A. Philip Randolph and Cyril Briggs, could not get the Negro church leaders to support their socialist-inspired campaigns for social change, therefore Negro religion must be conservative. Communist-influenced social scientists of the 1930s also characterized the Negro religion as conservative and otherworldly ("An opiate of the people"), when the institutional church failed to support openly Communist-led schemes and projects "for the race."[43]

Franklin correctly notes that "there was little attempt made to separate the political position assumed by Afro-American religious institutions and the belief-system within Afro-American Christianity." In that belief system, there is no inherent contradiction between "otherworldliness" and the struggle for justice in this world. To the enslaved people, for example, the most important escape Christianity offered was escape from the degraded identity imposed by the slave system. Their religion provided the basis for an independent moral identity. Moral identity, in turn, is the first prerequisite of sustained resistance to injustice.[44] In order to feel, unjustly treated people must first have a sense of their own worth. In light of this, they react against an unjust act as a violation and affront to their dignity. The slave system's intended dehumanization afflicted blacks who were unable to sustain such a moral identity. They became what the system intended them to be. Through black Christianity, however, the enslaved could short-circuit the dehumanizing process, and put themselves back in control of their own self-image. The relationship with God through Christ became the basis for identity, rather than the relationship with the enslaver or the enslaver's power. Whatever the character or pretensions of the earthly master, confidence in God's love made it possible for the enslaved to affirm their own worth, based on the knowledge that they were beloved of God.[45]

Through the idea of their relationship with God, the enslaved achieved a perspective that allowed them to feel that they existed in and for themselves, rather than through their relationship with the enslavers. This comes through clearly in the words and meaning of the spirituals, the moving songs of faith and religious passion that were the greatest artistic achievement of the enslaved. From *The Spirituals and the Blues*: "Heaven, in the black spirituals, was an affirmation of this hope in the absolute power of God's righteousness as revealed in God's future."[46] Against overwhelming odds, "black people fought the structures of slavery and affirmed their membership in a 'city whose builder and maker was God.' "[47] And "they welcomed God's judgment because it would uncover their new, true personhood. 'O, nobody knows who I am, till the judgment morning,' "[48] they sang.

V. P. Franklin notes: "The God of the Negro Spirituals and the enslaved Afro-Americans was a just God who would sit in judgment over all humanity, the high and the low, the good and the evil."

Just as you live,
Just so you die,
And after death,
Judgment will find you so.

O, brethren, brethren,
Watch and pray,
Judgment will find you so.
For Satan's round
You every day,
Judgment will find you so.[49]

The slave system treated the enslaved as instruments, stripped of the essential moral characteristic of human dignity, which demands that each human being be treated as an end. Through their faith the enslaved saw themselves with this dignity restored. This would explain the supposed anomaly in the content of the spirituals. As James Cone observed, in the spirituals

> . . . there is a surprising absence of references to white people as a *special* object of hate and scorn. One would expect indirect expressions of resentment, if not direct references. But aside from such songs as "Everybody talking about heaven, ain't goin' there" and "When I get to heaven goin' to sing and shout, there will be nobody to turn me out," the spirituals are strangely silent on the ethical behavior of the white masters. Most of them focus on the ethical responsibilities of members within the black community.[50]

Cone notes that some critics see this "as evidence that black slaves accepted their slave condition," but he rejects this idea in favor of the view that the enslaved people experienced such evil from whites that they simply "regarded white people as natural phenomena, like tornadoes, earthquakes, or floods,"[51] and excluded them from the realm of moral beings. However, this view implies that the enslaved simply relieved enslavers of moral responsibility for the evil they perpetrated. In fact, the opposite was closer to the truth. Cone observes, "The heaviest emphasis in the slaves' religion was on change in their earthly situation and divine retribution for the cruelty of their masters."[52] This appeared in folk tales as well:

> The most explicit and realistic portrayal of slavery appears in the John or Jack series. John . . . often defies his master and expresses a desire for revenge for his sufferings. In one tale John prays "for God to come git him [master] and take him to Hell right away because massa is evil." On another occasion Efram prays: "I'm tired staying here and taking these beatings. . . . Kill all the white folks and leave all the niggers."[53]

People don't seek revenge from tornadoes and earthquakes.[54]

Cone's error (surprising in a discussion that is in other respects remarkably insightful) results from his failure to consider the possibility that the absence of allusions to whites in the spirituals is just that, an indication that many of the spirituals represent the enslaved's communion with God without reference to their earthly captors. In an earlier part of his discussion of the spirituals, he comes close to seeing this possibility when he rightly concludes that "if black history were no more than the story of what whites did to blacks, there would have been no spirituals." But he fails to follow through on this thought when he goes on to say: "The primary reality is what blacks did to whites in order to delimit the white assault on their humanity." With this conclusion, Cone falls back into the slave system's view of the enslaved, which is that they have no existence or reality apart from their relationship with enslavers and their place in the slave system.[55] The enslaved themselves knew otherwise. They knew that their humanity had nothing to do with whites, that it was a cosmic reality grounded in nature and nature's God. Their spirituals and their religious faith were expressions of this knowledge. They could put aside the dialectic of master and slave, which the slave system sought to impose as the only reality. Through the spirituals, the prayers, the sermons, and distinctive rituals of their worship, they could express the capacity for transcendent contemplation of the whole, the capacity that is not just the mark but the true flower of human consciousness.

One of Cone's fellow black theologians, Gayraud Wilmore, rightly observed: "Black religion has always concerned itself with the fascination of an incorrigibly religious people with the mystery of God, but it has been equally concerned with the yearning of a despised and subjugated people with the freedom of man." What Cone, Wilmore, and other liberation theologians have failed to articulate adequately, however, is the essential connection between black Christianity's transcendental impulse and the will and courage to resist oppression. For the believing Christian, the relationship with God is the source of redemptive power in the world. In Christ, the mystery of God takes human form, a form that represents God's interest in the world and His love for the individuals in it. Christ is one person through whom the whole world is redeemed. Individual salvation is therefore bound up with that of the whole. Personal responsibility, prefigured by Christ's redemptive self-sacrifice, is, therefore, the key to Christian ethics. But Christ's Resurrection implies that Christians who imitate his sacrifice are beyond the realm of death,[56] and therefore beyond the domineering power of those who manipulate the fear of death. Rightly understood, then, the enslaved person's adherence to Christianity could, in and of itself, become a revolutionary fact, through which the enslaved accomplished the psychological subversion of the slave mentality.

It is no coincidence that Christian faith often formed the basis of a sustained commitment to fight the injustice of slavery, the kind of commitment that produced Nat Turner's rebellion[57] or Harriet Tubman's dedication to the work of liberating her enslaved brethren.[58]

Although information is limited, it is possible to draw a portrait of the Antebellum rebel leaders. For the most part, they were young, literate, married, charismatic men. Finding sanctions for their bloodletting in the Bible, inspiring the fainthearted with apocalyptic visions from the Scriptures of God delivering the Israelites from the hands of their oppressors, the leaders convinced the blacks that slavery was contrary to the will of God and that He commanded them to rise.[59]

. . . most of the active black leaders of abolitionism were related to churches. For example, the basement of the Mother Bethel A.M.E. Church in Philadelphia was used by Bishop

Richard Allen to hide escaped slaves, and numerous other black church leaders and their congregants risked their freedom and sometimes their lives to further the cause of freedom. However, the A.M.E. Zion Church became known as the freedom church because it was the spiritual home for some of the most famous of the legendary figures of the abolitionist movement: Frederick Douglass, Harriet Tubman, Sojourner Truth, Rev. Jermain Louguen, Catherine Harris, Eliza Ann Gardner, and Rev. Thomas James.[60]

Historians often cite the deep religiosity of the great figures of the black resistance as evidence that Christian faith is not incompatible with a spirit inflamed with the courage to fight injustice. Yet W.E.B. Du Bois's grimly eloquent description of Christianity's influence upon the slave continues to haunt the reputation of the black church.

Nothing suited his condition better than the doctrines of passive submission embodied in the newly learned Christianity. . . . The Negro, losing the joy of this world, eagerly seized upon the offered conceptions of the next; the avenging spirit of the Lord enjoining patience in this world, under sorrow and tribulation until the Great Day when He should lead His dark children home . . .[61]

Later, in his work on black religious ideas, Bernard Mays would reiterate views similar to those of Du Bois. Mays said that black religious ideas "encourage one to believe that God is in His heaven and all is right with the world," and that they

enable the Negroes to endure hardship, suffer pain, and withstand maladjustment, but they do not necessarily motivate them to strive to eliminate the source of the ills they suffer. . . . As God protected the Jews from Pharaoh, the Negro masses have believed that God in His good time and in His own way would protect and deliver them.[62]

It is probably true, as Franklin, Cone, and others have argued, that Mays's conclusions are based upon an overly superficial analysis of black spirituals, sermons, and other religious expressions, one that neglects the double meanings and encoded allusions the enslaved used to mask their more dangerous emotions from their oppressors. Yet can we deny that, as Du Bois says, the enslaved black had "elements in his character which made him a valuable chattel"? Can we deny that the vast majority of blacks labored patiently under the lash, daily compromising with the system that degraded them rather than rising against it to seek liberty or death? Isn't the criticism of black Christianity also an expression of shame or contempt for the patience under the yoke of the black millions who chose rather to live as slaves than die for freedom?[63]

In his work on politics, the ancient-Greek philosopher Aristotle correctly implies that enslavement is an extension of warfare.[64] Captured, disarmed, and transported far from their native lands, enslaved blacks were like prisoners of war, but cut off from any hope that the end of hostilities would bring release and a return to their homeland. Entirely in the power of their enemies, in an era when things like the Geneva convention were only a dream, they were given the choice to labor or die. Under such circumstances, what sense does it make to criticize them because they did not "strive to eliminate the source of the ills they suffer?" Did Americans taken prisoner by the Germans, the Japanese, the North Koreans, or the North Vietnamese strive to eliminate their captors? Does anyone shame them for their failure to do so? They tried to escape, and so did enslaved blacks. They tried to maintain, if only in some hidden form, the spark of resistance and inward humanity, and so did enslaved blacks. They strove to retain, against the pressures of torture and all the evils they endured, a sense of right and goodness that would leave them with some measure of their own worth other than the will of their captors. And so, through the medium of their Christian faith, did the blacks in slavery.

But knowing that no help was on the way, and that the whole burden of the war lay upon them, black Americans did much more. They lived out a strategy aimed at liberation. Like the Roman general who ultimately defeated Hannibal's military genius, they did not risk all in a few pitched battles they could not win. Instead, they resolved to wear down and outlast their enemy, avoiding his strengths, learning and exploiting his weaknesses, but never losing sight of their ultimate objective, never surrendering the spiritual resources that would give them the courage to strike when the time was right. With those resources intact, a people may lose a thousand battles, yet live on to claim the victory.

The black church is the spiritual storehouse of the black multitudes, and when the moment came, they were ready for it. Academics attacked black Christianity for fostering submissiveness. Communist and other leftist intellectuals criticized the black church for its lack of commitment to social change. Yet slavery is dead. Communism is dying. Legally enforced segregation and discrimination are things of the past, but the black church endures, and has once already led the way to genuine success in the struggle for justice. Though nothing in the critique of black Christianity helps us to understand it, the fact is that the one era of decisive progress for black Americans against racist laws and practices came about primarily through the leadership of the black church and the inspiration of black Christianity. The Civil Rights movement of the 1960s owed its success to the deep, enduring character of black Americans. Far more than the cultural expressions of the intellectual elite that has more or less openly despised it, the church–embodied faith of black Americans gave that character its winning strength.

Ezekiel saw a wheel,
Way up in the middle of the air.
Oh, Ezekiel saw a wheel,
Way up in the middle of the air.
The little wheel run by faith,
The big wheel run by the Grace of God.

Chapter 4

THOSE

WHO

WOULD

BE FREE

At various periods in our history, the proponents of slavery and racial repression have described blacks as subhuman, inherently inferior, congenitally immoral, and incapable of advancement beyond a certain level.[1] Such views figured in every effort to legitimize the system of racial oppression, from the harshest models of chattel slavery to the most benign paternalism. They portrayed blacks as beasts, as emotionally incontinent savages, as children capable of only limited responsibility, as mental inferiors incapable of education, culture, or economic independence. Such descriptions had a dual purpose. They aimed to justify, or at least confuse the issue of enslavement and repression in the eyes of conscientious whites. They also facilitated domination of blacks by assaulting their moral identity.

Whether enslaved or free, blacks have always resisted these demeaning characterizations, though in most cases, they could not do so in a direct, aggressive way. We have already seen what this meant in the context of the ideals of family life and religious aspiration. Blacks resisted the destruction of their family ties. They resisted the attempt to turn their religious impulse into an instrument of domination. Often this resistance meant great emotional and physical suffering, which they passively endured. Yet through this suffering, they achieved important moral victories. The persistence of the idea of family, and the development of autonomous black churches were the fruits.

The same strategy of nonviolent resistance can be seen in other aspects of life. During slavery, for example, laws as well as mores sought to discourage the enslaved from learning.[2] In 1850, Frederick Douglass could say with accuracy that "in every state of the American Union, where slavery exists, except the state of Kentucky, there are laws absolutely prohibitory of education among the slaves."[3] Yet some blacks pursued whatever avenues of learning they could, so that "literate slaves appeared everywhere, no matter how unfavorable the atmosphere."[4]

An important part of the oppression of enslavement was depriving Afro-Americans of knowledge of their condition, and thus the ways to change it. But the desire for literacy and "booklearning" was often stronger than the prohibitions and persecutions associated with the slave regime, and as a result, in so many difficult and diverse fashions, enslaved Afro-Americans learned to read and write.[5]

The few slaves who learned to read gained immeasurable status in the quarters because they had a secret mirror on the outside world and could keep the others informed of events which were transpiring there. . . . In addition, education elevated the slave's sense of personal worth in the midst of his afflictions. . . . Since whites put so many restrictions upon slaves obtaining an education, the slaves themselves invested it with almost magical qualities.[6]

Contrary to the contemporary presumption that only educated people transmit the value of education to their offspring, "it was often
the case that those who themselves were illiterate and unschooled
held firmest the value of 'education for advancement.' "[7] The thirst
for learning often carried a high price, since "mutilation (or death)
could sometimes result when enslaved Afro-Americans tried to become literate men and women."[8]

What was true for the enslaved was even more pronounced
among free blacks. In his work on the free blacks during the slavery
era, Ira Berlin offers a concise summary:

> Next to the church, the African school was the most impor-
> tant institution in the free Negro community. . . . Like whites,
> free Negroes believed education was a means of bettering
> themselves. . . . Education, however, was more than a means
> of self-improvement. A "good education," declared William
> Watkins, a leading Baltimore schoolmaster, "is the sine qua
> non as regards the elevation of our people."[9]

> There is little doubt that free Negroes were eager to secure
> an education. Of 2,038 in Boston in 1850, almost 1,500 were
> in school. There were 1,400 at school in Baltimore and 1,000
> in New Orleans. . . . In every community free Negroes were
> studying, with an apparent belief that education would solve
> some of their problems. Where opportunities did not exist,
> they sought to create them and gave enthusiastic support to
> their institutions.[10]

Berlin notes that the development of schools and churches often
went hand in hand. "Every African church had a Sunday school,
and most supported schools where black children attended classes
free or at a minimal charge."[11] In the North, black students also
had access to integrated public schools. In the slavery-dominated

South, however, free black efforts to obtain education or establish schools often faced determined white resistance.

> In many places, public hostility to educating Negroes and proscriptive laws prevented blacks from organizing schools even if they financed them on their own. Nevertheless, blacks risked imprisonment and the lash to keep their schools open. After Georgia prohibited the education of free Negroes, Julian Troumontaine, a free negro instructor of the Savannah African School, took his academy into hiding and continued to teach free Negro children until he was caught fifteen years later. Such clandestine schools could be found in almost every community that legally prohibited them.[12]

During the Reconstruction era, blacks continued to pursue their educational hopes by every available means. Many went to the freedmen's schools run by northern missionaries, black and white, and supported by northern philanthropy and some federal funds. Black churches expanded their efforts, extending the pattern of African-American schools among free blacks to include recently freed people. Such efforts were often financed out of the slim incomes of the newly freed blacks themselves.

The end of the Reconstruction period brought a resurgence of antiblack repression. So-called Redemptionist state governments in the South refused to provide fair and adequate funding for black education.

> It should come as no surprise that, lacking federal funds, and with the Afro-American population almost completely disenfranchised, and amid increasing black poverty and overt white hostility to black advancement, the public educational services and facilities made available to southern black (and white) children in 1900 and 1910 were in many ways inferior to those public services provided back in 1890.[13]

Yet, as V. P. Franklin notes, even given all these negative pressures, by 1910, "the masses of Afro-Americans had become more literate."[14]

Du Bois, U. S. Census Bureau officials, and others accepted as basically accurate the statistical fact that the 70 percent illiteracy rate (defined as inability to write) among Afro-Americans in 1880 had dropped to about 30 percent in 1910. In each decade between 1880 and 1910 the black population increased, but the number of illiterates in each age group decreased.[15]

With education as with the family, even though they had so much going against them, black Americans refused to surrender the values they had come to see as essential to their moral identity. Franklin acknowledges this when he concludes that "we must look to the 'cultural context' of literacy for Afro-America" when explaining this remarkable achievement. As we should expect by now, that context turns out to be the black church.

Thus many Afro-Americans learned to read and write in various religious settings, such as Sunday School classes and Sabbath Schools, within their own communities. Afro-American families not only preserved and passed on cultural values supporting education and social advancement, but also taught their children to read and write as part of the parental responsibility for the "Christian education" of the younger generation.[16]

Black perseverance in education, despite the obstacles of renewed repression during the Jim Crow era, is a prime example of nonviolent resistance. Starting in the 1880s, blacks experienced an era of wholesale repression. A pattern of violence, economic repression, and political disenfranchisement emerged throughout the South, where 90 percent of all black Americans still lived.

> During the past few years . . . the evidence that is beginning to accumulate suggests that the attack on the material con- ditions of the life of blacks after the Civil War was not only more ferocious, but, in certain respects, more cruel than that which preceded it. It appears that life expectations of blacks declined by 10 percent between the last quarter century of the antebellum era and the last two decades of the nineteenth century. The diet of blacks deteriorated. . . . The health of blacks deteriorated. . . . The skill composition of the black labor force deteriorated.[17]

> . . . many one-time crusaders against slavery sat idly by or even collaborated in passing various laws which served to im- prove the economic position of whites at the expense of blacks. Licensure laws helped to squeeze blacks out of some crafts. Educational restrictions helped to exclude them from others. Meanwhile, taxation and fiscal policies were used to transfer income from blacks to whites, perhaps more effec- tively, certainly more elegantly, than had been possible under slavery.[18]

Yet while the Ku Klux Klan and other racist vigilante groups burned, murdered, and terrorized blacks (as well as any whites who worked with them), the black community for the most part es- chewed violent responses. Black people concentrated instead on acquiring the knowledge they believed to be the key to advance- ment. In other areas or aspects of life, they placed the same em- phasis on self-improvement. They sought to acquire land for farming; they tried to learn and practice trades and crafts, and to establish businesses. In this they built on a tradition begun during the slavery era, when free blacks made precarious but significant economic progress despite the practices and prejudices working against them in all parts of the county.

Given the scale and depth of opposition they faced, it shouldn't surprise us that in general, these efforts couldn't reproduce the kind of success blacks scored in the pursuit of basic literacy. For our purposes, however, the important fact is not their success or failure, but the consistent purpose and strength of character they reveal. In this era, as during slavery, black Americans simply refused to allow their circumstances to dictate their identity or aspirations. They doggedly resisted the disheartening implications of repression. Instead, they fashioned from their circumstances a philosophy that committed blacks to the spirit of self-improvement, the very spirit their white racist enemies were working so hard to eradicate.

The much-maligned and misunderstood Booker T. Washington came to prominence during the era of Jim Crow repression because he articulated this philosophy of self-development for the masses.[19] He spoke for the ordinary majority of black people, the ones without special talents or abilities that set them apart. They were not yet in a position directly to challenge the structures of oppression arrayed against them, however much they hated and disapproved of them. But with dogged faith they held on to the moral ideals that formed the basis for black self-discipline and inner autonomy.

Washington translated this faith into a practical strategy for survival. He argued that American society had certain economic needs that had to be satisfied. Whether whites liked blacks or disliked them, Washington believed they would accept goods and services from qualified blacks capable of doing work of good quality. He emphasized in particular the acquisition of productive skills—carpentry and agriculture, for instance—which resulted in products that could stand on their own in the marketplace, and be judged without reference to the race or color of the craftsman. By trading on these products, blacks could build an economic foundation, despite the society's general prejudice against them.

In many respects, Washington's approach prefigured the ideas of black separatists, such as Elijah Muhammad, who came along much later. His compromise with segregation did not arise from a willingness to acknowledge or accept black inferiority. It reflected the traditionally strong black preference for self-sufficiency. He believed that blacks had to develop an economic base self-sufficient enough to allow them to live in their own communities without too much dependence on what whites did for them, or thought about them. However, unlike the separatists who sought a return to Africa, or the establishment of an independent black state or states on American soil, Washington thought that economic integration would make it possible to develop self-reliant black communities.

In his autobiography, Ralph David Abernathy describes the black community in which he grew up in terms that seem to correspond to Washington's vision.[20] Abernathy's father was a modestly successful black landowner and farmer. His self-sufficiency meant that his family could survive without much contact with whites, and without much experience of racial prejudice. It also allowed him to deal with whites on the basis of mutual respect. The Abernathy enclave was, of course, not an independent entity. Outside of it, the Abernathy children were still politically powerless and prey to racist insults. But it did apparently provide a secure enough foundation for Abernathy to develop a strong, positive sense of himself and his heritage.

Though Abernathy's experience was not the general rule for southern blacks, it suggests that Booker T. Washington's vision of black self-reliance was not simply a pipe dream. Until the Depression era, when general economic adversity and New Deal agricultural policies drove many black farmers off the land, a significant number of black landowners and tenant farmers achieved some version of the Abernathy model.[21] Others followed a tradition dating back to the free blacks and freedmen of the slavery era, and became skilled artisans—carpenters, shoemakers, caterers, etc. When increasing white prejudice and urbanization contributed to a decline in these areas, some blacks became successful entrepreneurs, serving the growing black population in predominantly black urban neighborhoods.[22] Of course, those who succeeded in this way did so in the face of enormous obstacles that kept their success from becoming a pattern for the black community at large. Despite Washington's efforts, the number of schools devoted to training blacks for economic development remained small. In many cases, lack of money and materials meant that they could not succeed in fully implementing the practical courses of study Washington envisaged.

Washington eventually came under fire from other black leaders because he advocated an educational approach for black youth that emphasized moral discipline and practical training. But when Frederick Douglass wrote to Harriet Beecher Stowe about the education blacks most needed, he outlined the philosophy Washington later put into practice:

> Accustomed, as we have been, to the rougher and harder modes of living, and of gaining a livelihood, we cannot, and we ought not to hope that, in a single leap from our low condition, we can reach that of Minister, Lawyers, Doctors, Editors, Merchants &c. These will, doubtless, be attained by us; but this will only be, when we have patiently and laboriously, and I may add successfully, mastered and passed through the intermediate gradations of agriculture and the mechanic arts.[23]

Douglass goes on to recommend the establishment "of an INDUSTRIAL COLLEGE in which shall be taught several important branches of the mechanical arts."[24] He reasons, as Washington would later, that "to live here as we ought we must fasten ourselves to our countrymen through their everyday cardinal wants. We must not only be able to black boots, but to make them."[25]

Though W.E.B. Du Bois later became one of Washington's most adamant critics, at one point, he expressed similar views on the best route to black advancement:

> Work, continuous and intensive work, although it be menial and poorly rewarded; work, though done in travail of soul and sweat of brow, must be so impressed upon Negro children as the road to salvation, that a child would feel it a greater disgrace to be idle than to do the humblest labor. The homely virtues of honesty, truth, and chastity must be instilled in the cradle, and although it is hard to teach self-respect to a people whose million fellow-citizens half despise them, yet it must be taught as the surest road to gain the respect of others.[26]

Such ideas probably came closest to articulating the strategy for survival most blacks pursued during the pre–Civil Rights period. They lacked the power to change the regime of repression and discrimination established against them. They had to survive. So they did what they could. They worked at the jobs that were open to them. They sacrificed so that at least one or two of their children could pursue some kind of education. They disciplined themselves to achieve, within the sphere allowed them, a decent life. And despite the odds against them, they survived. They went from being slaves to being struggling, working-class people, with an ethic of family cohesion and religious faith that guaranteed them a certain dignity.

The most numerous practitioners of this de facto Washingtonianism were black women. Though most never attended Washington's vocational schools, they nonetheless developed practical skills and offered them to the white community. They cooked, sewed, took in laundry, cleaned houses, and cared for children. Today, many people have contempt for these jobs, but for innumerable black families, they were the margin of survival or of progress beyond survival. Their work frequently brought them into contact with middle- and upper-class whites, so these black women also became the conduit for knowledge about their mores and values. With this knowledge, they could plant the seeds of higher ambitions in the hearts and minds of their children, while giving them a rough sense of the manners and outward appearances needed to pursue them. Black working-class women could operate as a kind of fifth column, behind the lines of the middle- and upper-class barriers that white racists adamantly refused to allow most blacks to cross.

Most discussions of black-American experience look for the expression of black values in writings and speeches of the relatively few black men who achieved prominence as thinkers and spokesmen of the race. Such discussions also consider the men who held forth from the pulpits, and eventually became the most visible leaders of the black Civil Rights movement. Yet in many respects, the moral and economic survival of the black community depended in large part on black women. While the ministers preached, they were the ones who kept the churches going on a daily basis. While the men faced, fought, and were often defeated by the many stratagems of racial discrimination, the women quietly slipped between the lines, earning money and developing a very practical understanding of what was needed to survive in a society dominated by whites.

Through the influence of such black working women, Washington's strategy of exploiting economic interdependence planted the seeds of social transformation. Though blacks remained poor in fact, and especially relative to the white population, poor did not automatically mean lower class. In matters of dress, speech, and public behavior, many black children acquired middle-class accents and manners. Of course, this education was not presented in terms of class. More often than not, it took place in the context of church activities, or the everyday interaction of grandmothers, mothers, or aunts with their young offspring or relations.

Black women were, of course, not the only practitioners of de facto Washingtonianism. Black men also took part in the working-class service economy, as janitors, butlers, elevator operators, doormen, Pullman-car porters, etc. In these positions as well, they acquired knowledge of the manners and mores of middle- and upper-class white society. Overall, therefore, though being black usually meant being poor, it did not necessarily mean the absence of other, noneconomic middle-class characteristics. In fact, when we combine the basic mores of the black community (family, faith, education) with the practical knowledge of middle-class behavior acquired by the black "fifth column," we get a black identity that has fairly complex class characteristics.

Decent working-class people laid the economic and social foundations that eventually produced both the Civil Rights movement and the larger black middle class that emerged in the period following its legislative successes. Unfortunately, though they formed the backbone of the black community, their complex class characteristics were often overlooked even by educated black observers. Because they provided needed services in areas whites were less inclined to enter, working-class blacks could find an economic niche despite white prejudice. Blacks seeking to break into more elite endeavors ran into that prejudice head on. Racist whites might accept having their food cooked by blacks, their houses cleaned, their shoes shined, their cars driven, etc., etc.—but they were much less likely to accept black lawyers, doctors, educators, or other professionals, since this meant working with and competing with blacks on an equal footing.

Paul Robeson's brief career with a New York law firm illustrates the problem perfectly. Robeson had been there a few weeks when a stenographer refused to take dictation from him, saying, "I never take dictation from a nigger." Robeson went to Louis Stotesbury, the partner who had offered him a position at the firm.

The two men discussed the situation frankly and fully. Stotesbury expressed admiration for Robeson's abilities but told him straight out that his prospects for a career in law were limited: the firm's wealthy white clients were unlikely ever to agree to let him try a case before a judge for fear his race would prove a detriment. Stotesbury said he might be willing to consider opening a Harlem branch of the office and put Robeson in charge of it, but Paul decided instead to resign. The profession of law, never that inviting, now seemed a decided dead end.[27]

White racism and segregation affected all blacks. But it had especially damaging effects on the pride and prospects of the black elite.

Working-class blacks could be both economically and psychologically more self-sufficient. They could grow their crops, ply their trade, or offer their services to white businesses and households without appearing to assimilate white cultural values, or aspiring to more extensive integration with their white clients and employers. As working-class people, they accepted work as a necessity. But even though bitter experience taught them that racism and discrimination would prevent them from getting a just return for their labor, this knowledge usually did not demoralize them, or lead them to interpret poverty as an indication of their own lack of dignity or self-worth. Though outwardly more submissive to racism, they actually had greater resistance to its demeaning implications. They could derive income from the white society, while living with self-respect within the confines of the separate black community enforced by segregation.

The more elite blacks could not. Psychologically, they felt a far greater need for white approval and acceptance than the black working class.[28] They had more completely assimilated white cultural values and practices. They therefore felt more deeply aggrieved when white society rejected them anyway. More vulnerable to racist insults and humiliation, they felt that the highest priority should be given to the struggle to obtain formal acknowledgment of equal rights and equal opportunities for blacks in American society. Du Bois's criticism of Booker T. Washington's philosophy reflected these class differences. He accused Washington of too passively accepting political disenfranchisement.[29] He also thought more emphasis had to be placed on achieving acknowledged equality with whites in all spheres of life.[30] Most important, he rejected Washington's emphasis on an educational strategy geared to the circumstances of the black masses:

> The Negro race, like all races, is going to be saved by its exceptional men. The problem of education, then, among Negroes, must first of all deal with the Talented Tenth; it is the problem of developing the Best of this race that they may guide the Mass away from the contamination and death of the Worst, in their own and other races.[31]

Du Bois's concern with the fate of elite blacks produced an agenda that focused on challenging white racism and the barriers to full black equality. He, and those who joined him in what was called the Niagara Movement in 1905, stressed the need for complaint, confrontation, and constant insistence on equality in all spheres. Though they acknowledged the importance of the development issues Washington stressed, they rejected the notion that economic progress could be achieved without a political base.

> Is it possible, and probable, that nine millions of men can make effective progress in economic lines if they are deprived of political rights, made a servile caste, and allowed only the

most meagre chance for developing their exceptional men? If history and reason give any distinct answer to these questions it is an emphatic *No*.[32]

In concrete terms, the Niagara Movement agenda insisted on full and immediate manhood suffrage; an end to racial segregation in public accommodation; and an end to social segregation and economic discrimination.[33] Racism is the chief enemy and preoccupation.[34] Integration, and even ultimate assimilation, is the goal whose achievement will signify that the enemy has been defeated. In the main, this became the agenda of the National Association for the Advancement of Colored People (NAACP) into which the Niagara Movement merged in 1910. In ideological terms, it represents the agenda that has dominated the black liberal establishment from that day to this.

Though it can be simply stated, this ideology in fact reflects the complex and often deeply conflicted personality of the black-American elite. The opposition to racial segregation was the result of injured pride, because segregation was based on the assumption of black racial inferiority. It was also the result of material injury, since racial discrimination meant inferior education, jobs, and living conditions for black people. The goal of integration was a result of prideful self-assertion, as opposed to humiliated acceptance of racial injustice. Yet it could also represent the view that a separate black identity was simply a negative fact, a consequence of oppression that was, by implication, a source of shame. In this sense, the goal of integration represents a reactionary mentality. Reacting against racial oppression, blacks define themselves and their goal strictly in terms of that oppression. But in this case, the symbol of oppression is separateness, the concrete representation in every phase of life of a separate black identity. How can one be thoroughly opposed to the evil without at least implicitly attacking the value of that separate identity? Yet by appearing to accept this implication, one validates the assumption of inferiority that is the really objectionable element in segregation. In the latter part of his life, Du Bois himself came to recognize this pitfall:

> The thinking colored people of the United States must stop being stampeded by the word *segregation.* The opposition to racial segregation is not or should not be any distaste or unwillingness of colored people to work with each other, to cooperate with each other, to live with each other. The opposition to segregation is an opposition to discrimination. . . . Our counterattack should be, therefore, against this discrimination. . . . But never in the world should our fight be against association with ourselves because by that very token we give up the whole argument that we are worth associating with.[35]

Unfortunately, the black liberal ideology was based on assumptions that made it hard to avoid the demeaning implications of the liberal agenda. In the first chapter of his book *The Negro Revolt,* Louis Lomax offers an analysis typical of the traditional, integrationist black liberal:

> The American Negro has been fashioned body, mind and spirit in the New World. Unlike other "minorities" in American society, we Negroes do not share a positive sense of identity. Alas, the only thing one Negro has exclusively in common with another Negro is the animus of the white man. . . . We cannot change our color; instead our efforts have been directed toward achieving what must be called "cultural whiteness," although we and our ancestors made substantial contributions to that culture. . . . The Negro individual has no hope of final and secure identification except with the general American social structure. And so it is that the American Negro is the only American who, as an individual, must reach beyond his own group for absolute identification. . . .

Negro history is but our continuing efforts to escape the
boundaries placed upon us by the white majority . . .[36]

(When people ask me why I am not a liberal, I refer them to this
passage and ask them to consider why any self-respecting black
American would want to be identified with such a self-degrading
ideology. The answer has to be ignorance of its true logical
foundations.)

. . . the motivation that drives the Negro grows out of a set
of values which emphasize the individual's worth, not his ethnic background. When we Negroes think racially it is because
we have been herded together whether we, as individuals,
belong together or not; the ambition of the Negro individual,
then, is to get the hell out of the Negro ghetto, be it physical
or mental, as soon as he can.[37]

Lomax's negative view of black history leads to a negative concept of the African-American identity. He implies that, whereas
Italians or Jews might see their ethnicity as an element of their
individual worth, African Americans see no positive value in their
group life and heritage. We have seen at previous points in our
discussion that Frazier, Du Bois, and Martin Luther King were all
influenced by the negative black historiography and sociology that
characterized their educations. At best, they learned to see the
black experience as the history of racism or racial oppression in
America. In this view, blacks appear as passive victims, as the objects of action rather than as actors in their own right. In principle,
though, this means that if the history has a positive outcome, if we
vanquish racism, there will no longer be a role in the American
drama for black Americans as such. In a chapter of his book called
"Pain and Progress," Lomax discusses this implication. He looks
forward to the day when Negro institutions, leaders, and newspa-
pers will no longer exist as such:

The Negro college, the Negro press, the Negro politician and the Negro church all have this flaw in common: they were born into a segregated world and set out to serve us with the view that our separate world would someday be equal. As a result, each of these, in a different way, has a stake in the [segregated] status quo. . . .[38] In time . . . Negro politicians will assume a new stance; they will be public servants, not Negros.[39]

The Negro press as a whole is walking a tightrope. To date they have been successful in reflecting the interests of their readers, but this success has been due largely to the assumption that there is a separate "Negro" audience with special interests that can be appealed to and exploited. This is true now, but there will come a time when the Negro revolt will make it less true.[40]

The key factor in the future of all these people and organizations—the Negro politician, the Negro press, the Negro schoolteacher, the Negro church—is whether they will be able to make the shift from ethnic to general institutions.[41]

Lomax's views clearly represent the self-defeating trap that Du Bois eventually recognized and feared. Lomax defines the revolutionary implications of the struggle for justice in such a way that they include the destruction of any separate African-American identity. This means that black Americans cannot aim blows against racism without dealing a fatal blow to their own existence as a people. More important, the belief that the black identity has no positive content means that, in dealing with the problems of the black community, one neglects to think about policies based on the community's internal values, institutions, and resources. Instead, one assumes that the solutions must come from without. The passive victims of history become the passive beneficiaries of philanthropy, the passive clients of bureaucracy, the passive subjects of the domineering welfare state. Despite all good intentions to the contrary, this type of liberalism pushes black Americans back toward a condition of endless childhood, servitude, and subjection. Liberal hope becomes liberal slavery.[42]

The fundamental choice facing black America has usually been presented as a choice between confrontation and accommodation, with Booker T. Washington as the siren of accommodation, and W.E.B. Du Bois the prophet of confrontation and resistance. If black Americans accept this way of seeing things, however, we remain trapped in the dialectic of racism, in terms of which our identity is defined entirely by racial categories and relationships. Is the first challenge before black Americans to defeat white racism or define and develop ourselves? For nearly three decades now, we have followed leaders whose rhetoric and policies derive from a preoccupation with the first issue. The second question has always seemed the province of fringe groups or advocates of violence— the black nationalists and separatists whom the majority of blacks applaud, admire, and refuse to join. The liberals seem to insist that we give up our claim to be black; the separatists, that we surrender our claim to be American. Yet in our hearts we know that the struggle to conserve both has been, as Du Bois sensed, our special destiny.

> One ever feels his twoness—an American, a Negro; two souls, two thoughts, two unreconciled strivings; two warring ideals in one dark body, whose dogged strength alone keeps it from being torn asunder. The history of the American Negro is the history of this strife—this longing to attain self-conscious manhood, to merge his double self into a better and truer self. In this merging he wishes neither of the older selves to be lost.[43]

Is there any hope in this struggle? As things stand today, we must be tempted to answer pessimistically. Du Bois and his Niagara Movement cohorts fashioned an agenda based on the belief that racial prejudice and legal segregation kept blacks from their American identity. Thanks to the success of the Civil Rights movement in the sixties, most of the Niagara Movement's originally stated goals have been achieved. Yet the triumph against legal segregation has lately begun to seem a Pyrrhic victory. Blacks living in the urban war zones, subject to the violent tyranny of the crime lords or the bureaucratic despotism of the welfare state, are bereft of and reject their American identity. Rap artists like Public Enemy or Sister Souljah bespeak their alienation. Their world of crime, drugs, cultural bravado, and moral disintegration is treated by the "opinion leaders" and social scientists as if it somehow represents the essence of the black identity. Therefore, relatively successful black Americans, the ones who work hard, pray hard, and keep their families going, find new reasons to shrink from their ethnicity. They resist the new forms of moral annihilation just as their ancestors resisted the old. Du Bois's vision of "two warring ideals in one dark body" appears at another level to be a community perpetually divided against itself in body, mind, and spirit. Even our progress seems to have aggravated this division.

Yet in the methods used to achieve that progress, haven't we already seen the key to overcoming our divided self? Our enslaved ancestors preserved their moral integrity by building their inward identity on a foundation that transcended their relationship with their oppressors. Martin Luther King successfully mobilized the black community by drawing upon our faith in a transcendent idea of justice. In both cases, blacks realized that they should not allow what they suffered to define who they were, or what they aimed to achieve. They did not allow the fact of slavery and oppression to define their identity as a people.

In its preoccupation with racism, the liberal tradition founded (though later abandoned) by Du Bois strayed from this principle. By accepting racism as the epitome of the black problem, the liberals made race the defining term of the black identity. Oddly enough, a traditional black liberal like Louis Lomax was perfectly capable of avoiding this when he looked at another ethnic group:

> Jews are white people, but orthodox, or conformist, Jews are more than just white; they are a people with a tradition . . . Of all the ethnic suburban ghettos . . . the Jewish communities were the most adamant about keeping Negroes out. Jewishness, not prejudice, is the explanation for this.[44]

Lomax recognized the difference between Jewish ethnocentrism and white racism. Why wouldn't the same difference apply to black Americans? In the dialectic of racism, the group identity may be a negative category. But in the objective truth of black history and experience, it becomes a positive fact, the accrued result of the values, institutions, and achievements of the black people who lived it. Seen in this way, racism becomes the context, rather than the subject of black-American history. It is the background against which blacks have defined themselves as a people. The struggle to survive in the face of this evil produces, as a positive result, a people with the admixture of virtue and vice, faith and cynicism, spiritual clarity and moral confusion that makes black Americans what they are. This view takes account, too, of the reality that the term *black* or *African American* encompasses people of many different racial mixtures: African, European, Native American, and Asian stock are all mingled together, often by acts of violence, sometimes by acts of love that braved all violence. Contrary to the assumptions of racism, people are not defined by their physical characteristics. A people can define itself, however, through the values that make possible its physical, moral, and spiritual survival. We know already that black Americans developed such values. But until now, this development was seen as a response to racism, as if the whole black effort and experience consists in proving that white prejudices are wrong. Yet whether we are winning or losing the battle against prejudice and repression, this moral heritage remains. Regardless of what other people think or do, the values black Americans developed define the common ground of our identity, which is always on offer as a basis for our communal life.

David had a harp, had one string
Just one string
Made the whole heaven ring.
Saul said to David:
Come play me a piece.
David said to me:
How can I play
When I'm in a strange land?
L'il David, play on your harp, Allelu, Allelu,
L'il David play on your harp, Allelu.

Chapter 5

THAT'S

GOT

HIS

OWN

W hen we black Americans think of ourselves mainly in terms of our relations with whites, we argue and are divided among ourselves. When we think instead in terms of our obligation to ourselves, we find a broad measure of agreement and common ground. We had to cope with a system of repression designed to focus on race relations, to define our progress as progress in race relations. Of course, since the racial problem has been mainly the result of white attitudes and actions, this has meant that whites determined the significance of black achievement. From this perspective, the test of black advancement is not what blacks achieve, but the effect their achievements have on white attitudes.

Paul Robeson is a good example of what could happen to blacks trapped by this mentality. Robeson had the intelligence, ability, and education to be a fine lawyer. But since this achievement had no apparent effect on white attitudes, it had no significance for him. He found acceptance among whites as an actor and singer. Therefore, he defined singing and acting as real achievements, putting aside the law. Thurgood Marshall entered law practice during the same era when Robeson faced his choice. Marshall faced the same prejudices. Unlike Robeson, however, Marshall saw achievement in terms of his obligation to himself and the black community. Robeson rejected the idea of a law practice among blacks in Harlem. Marshall embraced the idea of practicing law on behalf of blacks in Baltimore. In the end, while Robeson angrily defied American opinion, Marshall succeeded in changing it.

As his subsequent career proves, Marshall's choice did not mean that he ignored white racial prejudice. He simply did not allow it to dominate his judgment about the value of his actions. His achievement—becoming a lawyer—had value because he could use it on behalf of black people. Black need, rather than white opinion, guided his career choice. The fact that whites despised his legal abilities did not, in his eyes, destroy their importance. On the contrary, it simply proved there was a great need for them.

As long as a black person believes that his actions derive value from their effect on white prejudices, those prejudices decide his actions. His future depends on what whites do, on what whites think, on how whites behave. Racism triumphs over everything that he does in this frame of mind, even when his actions are explicitly directed against it. Real liberation from racism comes with the realization that what whites think of blacks, or do to blacks, is less important than what we think of, and do for, ourselves.

We catch glimpses of this insight in some form in the writings and speeches of black thinkers who otherwise have very different views. Emigrationists who believed blacks should return to Africa; separatists who sought a separate state or "nation within a nation" in America; assimilationists who saw black Americans inseparably bound to the future of their American homeland—all appear to agree in the view Frederick Douglass summarized in an article in 1848:

It is evident that we can be improved and elevated only just so fast and far as we shall improve and elevate ourselves. We must rise or fall, succeed or fail, by our own merits. If we are careless and unconcerned about our own rights and interests, it is not within the power of all the earth combined to raise us from our present degraded condition. "Hereditary bondmen, know ye not,/Who would be free themselves must strike the blow?"[1]

Douglass was one of those who believed that black Americans had no home or future but in America. His one-time associate, Martin Delany, became a strong advocate of colonization, the establishment of a black homeland in Africa or Central America. Yet when writing on this subject in 1852, he expressed a similar view of the need for black self-reliance:

Our elevation must be the result of *self-efforts*, and work of our own hands. No other human power can accomplish it. If we but determine it shall be so, it will be so. Let each one make the case his own, and endeavor to rival his neighbor, in honorable competition.[2]

Despite the differences between them, Washington and Du Bois could also find common ground in this theme. In 1896, Washington wrote that "in working out our destiny, while the main burden and center of activity must be with us, we shall need in a large measure the help, the encouragement, the guidance that the strong can give the weak." In the conclusion of his work on the Philadelphia Negro, Du Bois wrote much the same:

Modern society . . . can rightly demand that as far as possible and as rapidly as possible the Negro bend his energy to the solving of his own social problems. . . . For the accomplishment of this the Negro has a right to demand freedom for self-development, and no more aid from without than is really helpful for furthering that development. Such aid must of necessity be considerable . . . but the bulk of the work of raising the Negro must be done by the Negro himself, and the greatest help for him will be not to hinder and curtail and discourage his efforts. Against prejudice, injustice and wrong the Negro ought to protest energetically and continuously, but he must never forget that he protests because those things hinder his own efforts and that those efforts are the key to his future.[3]

Aside from black churches, Marcus Garvey's movement in the 1920s was the only effort that won active participation from the black masses. Garvey unashamedly subscribed to the racialism that dominated the social thought of his day. "I believe," he declared, "that white men should be white, yellow men should be yellow and black men should be black in the great panorama of races. . . . The white man of America will not, to any organized extent, assimilate the Negro, because in so doing he feels that he will be committing racial suicide."[4] Though Garvey places it in the context of racial reaction (i.e., "breaking down prejudice"), he too raised the common theme of self-reliance:

The Negro must be up and doing if he will break down the prejudice of the rest of the world. Prayer is not going to improve our condition nor the policy of watchful waiting. We must strike out for ourselves in the course of material achievement, and by our own effort and energy present to the world those forces by which the progress of man is judged.[5]

The common sense of black thinkers about the need for economic self-development didn't stop at exhortation. Though it was never implemented, in the 1920s, Du Bois articulated a comprehensive scheme for black economic self-sufficiency.[6] During the same period, Marcus Garvey tried to implement race-based, but thoroughly capitalist, enterprises, including "cooperatives, factories, a commercial steamship venture, the Black Star Line. . . ."[7] The conclusion seems justified that "these enterprises were complete failures because of incompetence, mismanagement, and other difficulties."[8] Yet by their thousands, ordinary working people in the black community showed, with their financial contributions, their faith in the idea of black economic self-sufficiency Garvey articulated. Between 1919 and 1921, he reportedly collected nearly ten million dollars to support his ambitious plans.[9] The idea of economic self-reliance was also a natural adjunct of Booker T. Washington's philosophy of market-oriented education. He became one of its most successful promoters.

> No organization was as influential in stimulating the philosophy of self-help and racial solidarity as the National Negro Business League, which Washington organized in 1900 to encourage the development of Negro business. . . . So successful was the league that 1200 attended its 1906 meeting at Atlanta. At this meeting the delegates in typical Tuskegee spirit reaffirmed their faith in the progress that the race had made and could make in business, declared their belief that like all races Negroes must depend for their elevation mainly on their ability to make progress in constructive, visible directions by laying a foundation in economic growth. . . .[10]

The emphasis on black self-reliance did not mean that these leaders rejected help or cooperation from others. Even Garvey welcomed "the voluntary help and appreciation of that class of other races that is reasonable, just and liberal enough to give each and every one a fair chance. . . ."[11] Washington relied on help from Andrew Carnegie, Julius Rosenwald, and other white philanthropists. Oswald Garrison Villard and other liberal white financial backers funded Du Bois and the NAACP. So the key element of self-reliance wasn't racial exclusivity, but responsibility. Investment, cooperation, and patronage could come from anywhere, but in the struggle for their own advancement, black Americans had to accept the prime responsibility for success or failure. Black advocates and practitioners of self-reliance believed that, as a practical imperative, only blacks themselves could provide a consistent foundation[12] for black advancement. In the economic sphere, this led to an approach that stressed group solidarity—black support for black enterprises—on the way to developing the ability to function effectively in the general American market.[13]

In its most comprehensive form, the pursuit of self-reliance led to efforts to establish entirely black communities, which combined economic self-sufficiency with social and political autonomy.

These were an institutionalized expression, in extreme form, of the ideological patterns of self-help and racial solidarity. Such communities had existed since ante-bellum times, but their heyday began during the 1880's. Though many efforts were abortive, a significant number of such settlements were created.[14]

These efforts appear "extreme," however, only because of the connection between slavery and the presence of blacks in the New World. During the colonial era, ethnic settlements were in fact the norm. Beside the English settlements, there were Dutch settlements in New York, German communities in Pennsylvania and Ohio, French communities in Louisiana, Swedish settlements in Wisconsin, and so forth. Thanks to the attitudes engendered by the slave culture, however, what was taken for granted in other groups as a normal expression of the desire for group autonomy and local self-government could appear to be extreme in African Americans. Prejudice declared blacks naturally suited to be slaves. This meant, as Aristotle argued long ago, that they were incapable of self-government. Blacks who sought to establish self-governing local communities acted in accordance with general American traditions, but they violated the most basic tenet of the racist ideology used to legitimize the enslavement and abuse of black people.

Though they can hardly be called representative, black efforts to achieve local self-government symbolized the common idea that appears as we interweave the disparate strands of African-American political and social thought. The struggle for liberation is not just a struggle to be free of the master. The aim is, as Douglass said, to be your own master. This requires a material foundation. Hence the common-sense emphasis on economic development. It also implies the ability to make crucial decisions for yourself as an individual, which is why black thinkers considered education and moral character so vitally important to black progress. Ultimately, though, being your own master involves the ability to participate authoritatively in the governance of the community in which you live. This is what Du Bois and others fought for when they emphasized the struggle for voting rights. It's what William Benson and E. P. McCabe sought when they established self-governing black towns. It's what Garvey and Blyden sought when they advocated building a black nation in Africa.

The emphasis on work, education, and self-advancement reflected the values of the overwhelming majority of black Americans. Yet they pursued them without adopting any of the specific agendas promoted by leaders and intellectuals. At the communal level, it was once again through the black church that the masses first demonstrated their commitment to self-reliance and self-government. The churches "are of particular importance . . . because in view of their mass base, their activities probably reflect the thinking of the inarticulate majority better than any other organizations or the statements of editors and other publicists."[15] We have already discussed the crucial role of the churches in black educational pursuits. In addition, through the churches blacks organized the burial and mutual-aid societies that later evolved into banks and insurance companies. These were just the formal manifestation of the network of informal self-help activities that usually went on within churches. Church organizations for men, women, and youth provided an informal welfare structure, extending aid to older members who could no longer do for themselves, to families in trouble because of the sickness or death of a breadwinner, to children in need of foster care.[16]

Separate black churches emerged in the first place because black Americans wanted greater autonomy and respect than they were accorded in predominantly white congregations. Though partly a response to white prejudice, they became the chief institutional embodiments of black self-respect and mutual cooperation. Southern black rural churches were often in fact simply incarnations of the extended family group.

As blacks migrated to the cities, this became the basis for the concept of church community that prevailed in many urban churches. Larger black communities in urban areas meant larger church membership, and correspondingly greater resources. Therefore, it offered a larger pool of educated and worldly-wise members. As the black population became more urbanized, welfare and self-help activities outside the church grew in importance.

> Du Bois, reviewing developments down to 1909, found Negroes engaged in general charity, women's clubs, libraries, day nurseries, kindergartens, and settlement houses. The most successful work was being done in old folks' homes and orphanages, of which there were fully a hundred by 1913, almost all of them dating from the 1890's or later. Social settlements and nonprofit hospitals appeared in the 1890's. Though these obtained their chief support from whites, they were ordinarily promoted and conducted by Negroes and were therefore regarded as examples of self-help.[17]

Though organized formally outside the black church structure, such activities were usually motivated by Christian beliefs and values. They were often initiated or inspired by church members, or else emerged from church-based activities as people sought to pool their resources and efforts across denominational lines. They often drew upon church facilities and networks for support.

The pervasive role of the black church, both in material terms and as a community of values, blurred the distinction between secular and religious activities in the black community. This explains the importance black Americans attached to political activity within the church.

The Negro church was not only an arena of political life for the leaders of Negroes, it had a political meaning for the masses. Although they were denied the right to vote in the American community, within their churches, especially the Methodist Churches, they could vote and engage in electing their officers. The elections of bishops and other officers and representatives to conventions has been a serious activity for the masses of Negroes.[18]

The choice of church leaders was important because, for all practical purposes, black churches became the vehicle of community self-government for black Americans. Church leaders controlled access to the church network not only for church activities but for all other activities that required community support and involvement.[19] Whenever black Americans wanted to organize anything, the church was the starting point. During the segregation era, this was due in part to the fact that churches often represented the only facilities for meetings and social gatherings easily accessible to blacks. But it was also because the church was the most reliable "public square" for the community, the place where one could be sure to find and communicate with both the community's leadership and the mass of its citizens.

This led to and explains the important role of churches in the Civil Rights movement. Even before the era of boycotts, marches, and demonstrations, the church network provided most of the grassroots leadership and support for the NAACP, especially in the South. When the community turned to a strategy of direct action to supplement the NAACP's focus on legal or administrative remedies for discrimination, churches provided the main organizational muscle and a sustaining flow of financial resources. Even acknowledging the contributions of campus-based student organizations, it's fair to say that the Civil Rights movement was a church-based, faith-inspired movement, much like the abolitionist cause in the nineteenth century.

Sometimes individuals face a time of great crisis or great opportunity, a time that it seems they have prepared for their whole lives. All their emotional and psychological resources, their strengths and their weaknesses, come into play. Their deepest beliefs and convictions are tested against the challenge. These are the moments of birth and rebirth that reveal their true identity. At such times, a person's character stands out most clearly against the background of his existence. For black Americans, the Civil Rights era was such a moment in our life as a people.

Before people can put together the means to do something, they must have the will to do it. Given the insidiously demoralizing effects intended by the race based system of slavery and oppression under which they had to live, black Americans should have become a broken, dispirited, and demoralized people. Instead, they proved to be a people capable of inspiring moral conviction and reformation in the very nation that oppressed them. This inspiration came especially from the exemplary courage, dignity, and determination of the people themselves—the people who chose not to ride the buses, so that public transportation boycotts in places like Baton Rouge, Jacksonville, and Montgomery would be effective; the people who found a few dollars in their too-meager incomes to support the carpool systems that allowed boycotts to continue; the people who braved the hoses and attack dogs, the bombings and snipers in the night, to sit in, march, and demonstrate once and for all that America would have no peace until racial injustice ceased.

Under the influence of Max Weber's well-known theory of charismatic leadership, popular conceptions of the Civil Rights movement tend to emphasize the role of leaders like Martin Luther King, Jr.[20] Yet what King represented and forcefully articulated before the nation and the world was essentially a decentralized, grassroots phenomenon. It relied, for its leadership and the core of its financial resources, on local, usually church-based, institutions and organizations in communities throughout the South. King did not create the movement. Rather, he became for a time the prime focus of its ideas and actions. Acting as a prism for the various shades of feeling and opinion among black Americans, he blended them into a common appeal in which all blacks could see themselves, and all Americans could see the nation's better destiny.

King's message is therefore important to us not just for what it says, but for what it says about the character of the people whose values and aspirations he represented. An appeal that evokes a positive response in one community may fall flat in another, depending on the character of the people involved. People dominated by greed will applaud an appeal that promises riches. People motivated by the thirst for power and dominion approve an appeal that promises conquest and empire. When Martin Luther King spoke to gatherings of black Americans, when he sought words with which to express what motivated and sustained them, he looked for themes, symbols, and ideas he thought they would embrace. The popularity of his leadership proves that he found what he was looking for. Though he adopted an approach that placed great demands on the courage and self-discipline of his followers, he did not find them wanting. This was in large part because the black church community from which he came and on which he relied was not only a community of need and suffering. It was a community of values, and of people used to acting for the sake of those values every day, against a world of opposition.

Throughout King's speeches, sermons, and writings, three principles predominate: justice, nonviolence, and love. Justice is the end, nonviolence the means, and love the motive. Yet, as in the trinitarian concept of God in Christianity, these three principles appear to be different aspects of one indivisible idea. Love turns out to be the inner substance of justice,[21] nonviolence its outwardly visible expression. Together they represent the moral reality that transcends the material world, but ultimately determines what happens within it.

> . . . the method of nonviolence is based on the conviction that the universe is on the side of justice. It is this deep faith in the future that causes the nonviolent resister to accept suffering without retaliation. He knows that in his struggle for justice he has cosmic companionship. This belief that God is on the side of truth and justice comes down to us from the long tradition of our Christian faith.[22]

> I think every person who believes in nonviolent resistance believes somehow that the universe in some form is on the side of justice. That there is something unfolding in the universe . . . that unfolds for justice, and so in Montgomery we felt somehow that as we struggled we had cosmic companionship. And this was one of the things that kept the people together, the belief that the universe is on the side of justice.[23]

> One may well ask: "What is the nonviolent resister's justification for this ordeal to which he invites men, for this mass political application of the ancient doctrine of turning the other cheek?" The answer is found in the realization that unearned suffering is redemptive.[24]

Like his enslaved ancestors, King derives the strength of his moral identity from his trust in the power of God, and from a sense that he and those who suffer with him enjoy a special relationship with that power. The conviction King here expresses derives clearly and explicitly from the transcendental impulse, the "otherworldliness," of black Christian faith. But far from inducing passivity or sapping the will to resist, he makes clear that it provided the basis for unity and perseverance during the Montgomery bus boycott, the black community's organized protest against racial discrimination in the public transit system in Montgomery, Alabama.

King believed that he had borrowed the concept of nonviolent resistance from Gandhi's example in South Africa and India. King also believed that nonviolent resistance marked a break with a past in which black Americans ". . . came to feel that perhaps they were less than human" and "the Negro . . . accepted the 'place' assigned him . . ."[25] As we have seen already, this view reflected the inadequate understanding of black-American history that prevailed in his day. Given what we now know of the culture and values of black Americans, during and in the aftermath of slavery, it's clear that King's philosophy and methods drew upon and developed what had already existed. His greatness lies in the fact that, at a historically propitious moment, he emerged to draw out and apply the resources black Americans had stored up in the treasure house of their spirit through centuries of enslavement and repression. Thus, by contrast with Gandhi, King did not have to invent new terms with which to convey the concept to his fellow African Americans. He did not have to create a spirit of nonviolence in his followers by making himself its living symbol. He relied on the language, symbols, and traditions of his African-American Christian heritage. His rhetoric evoked an immediate response in the black community because those traditions embodied the very concepts he sought to articulate. As we have seen, black Americans already believed in the transcendent basis and reality of justice. They already understood the redemptive meaning of suffering. When King staunchly defended the nonviolent method, he was, in fact, describing the approach that enslaved blacks used to thwart the dehumanizing intention of the slave system.

It must be emphasized that nonviolent resistance is not a method for cowards; it does resist. . . . It is not a method of stagnant passivity. The phrase "passive resistance" often gives the false impression that this is a sort of "do-nothing method" in which the resister quietly and passively accepts evil. But nothing is further from the truth. For while the nonviolent resister is passive in the sense that he is not physically aggressive toward his opponent, his mind and emotions are always active, constantly seeking to persuade his opponent that he is wrong. The method is passive physically, but strongly active spiritually.[26]

When King outlined the reasons for rejecting a more violent approach, he summarized the strategic dilemma of black Americans perfectly. The pitfall of the violent approach wasn't the physical danger involved.

The greatest danger is that it will fail to attract Negroes to a real collective struggle . . . it will mislead Negroes into the belief that this is the only path and place them as a minority in a position where they confront a far larger adversary than it is possible to defeat in this form of combat. When the Negro uses force in self-defense he does not forfeit support . . . his struggle will not be free of violence initiated by his enemies, and he will need ample courage and willingness to sacrifice to defeat this manifestation of violence. But if he seeks it and organizes it, he cannot win. Does this leave the Negro without a positive method to advance?[27]

King's argument suggests that if blacks put their faith in the violent approach, they would, in effect, be agreeing to fight on their enemy's terms. They would subject the hope that is the primary source of their moral strength to the outcome of a physical conflict in which, by design, they are at a disadvantage. If they failed (and history and their circumstances gave them every reason to believe they would), the belief that violent resistance was the only alternative would mean utter demoralization. Physical defeat would mean moral annihilation. This result is, in fact, precisely what those who structured the system of racial oppression aimed to achieve.

King's genius lay in realizing that black Americans could win decisive victories against racial oppression only by moving the battle from the physical to the moral plane. On that terrain, blacks enjoyed decisive superiority. On that terrain, physical defeats became the basis for moral victory and revitalization. The key to this strategy was King's realization that the principal weapons and fortresses in the struggle were in the *minds and hearts* of those engaged in it, on both sides.

. . . the nonviolent resister does not seek to humiliate or defeat the opponent but to win his friendship and understanding. . . . A boycott is never an end within itself. It is merely a means to awaken a sense of shame within the oppressor . . .[28]

Men are not easily moved from their mental ruts or purged of their prejudiced and irrational feelings. . . . So the nonviolent approach does not immediately change the heart of the oppressor. It first does something to the hearts and souls of those committed to it. It gives them new self-respect; it calls up resources of strength and courage they did not know they had. Finally, it reaches the opponent and so stirs his conscience that reconciliation becomes a reality.[29]

King's philosophy of nonviolent resistance applied at the tactical level a basic premise of the black strategy for survival in a hostile land. As King said, "In the history of the movement for racial advancement, many creative forms have been developed . . ." He goes on to list "the mass boycott, sit-down protests and strikes, sit-ins

—refusal to pay fines and bail for unjust arrests—mass marches—mass meetings—prayer pilgrimages, etc." He could also have listed the schools, self-help organizations, conventions, business leagues, and myriad other activities black Americans pursued in the effort to advance themselves.

The strategy of nonviolent resistance did not begin with the Civil Rights movement. King found a people prepared to succeed with it because they had survived with it for so long. The success they achieved reveals and confirms the real essence of the black-American ideal of self-reliance. Whatever its material or economic manifestations, for black Americans, it has meant especially reliance on our spiritual and moral resources. These defined the "self" on which, above all, black Americans learned to rely. Built firmly on the three pillars of family, faith, and a persistent commitment to self-improvement, our strong moral identity thwarted and eventually overcame the harmful strategems of racial prejudice and discrimination, as it had the racist system of enslavement.

Yet since the era of the Civil Rights movement's great triumphs over legalized discrimination, though individual blacks have progressed and prospered in significant numbers, the community as a whole has deteriorated. One great pillar of our identity, the family, is crumbling. A growing number of blacks in the so-called "underclass" have, for all practical purposes, abandoned the ethic of self-advancement. Black churches grow in membership even as they decline in moral influence and effect. The violence blacks once suffered at the hands of others many now inflict upon each other, in the schools, in the streets, in the womb, on such a scale that it amounts to self-administered genocide.

We will not understand what to do about this crisis until we have better understood how it came about. Our work so far clearly refutes the notion that this crisis is a necessary consequence of our heritage of slavery and repression. Those experiences did not kill us. In fact, in our responses to them, we forged our greatest strengths. We became skilled fighters in the spiritual resistance movement from which our moral identity emerged. Yet today, it is precisely the loss of a strong, positive moral identity that leaves so many of our young people vulnerable to the vicious temptations of drugs, crime, idleness, and promiscuity. Why is this happening? How has it come to pass? What can we do to turn back the swelling tide of dissolution and hopelessness?

I couldn't hear nobody pray,
I couldn't hear nobody pray,
Way down yonder, by myself,
And I couldn't hear nobody pray.

Chapter 6

OF JESSE
JACKSON
AND
OTHERS

L istening to black leaders today, it is hard to recognize the special moral identity of black Americans, as it has emerged in our discussion thus far. They have strayed too far from the values that form the essence of the black-American character. Though the suggestion may make them bristle with indignation, their alienation from the basic values of black America was at no time more apparent than during their unsuccessful attempt to block the nomination of Clarence Thomas to the Supreme Court. The Congressional Black Caucus, Jesse Jackson, and the national leaders of the NAACP, as well as other representatives of the black establishment, strongly opposed Thomas. In their zeal to block his elevation, they even accepted without demurral a prurient spectacle that played upon the most defamatory, racist slurs about black sexuality. Yet throughout the nomination process, including the rank indecency of the televised Senate hearings on Anita Hill's accusations, a solid majority of black Americans indicated to pollsters that they believed Thomas should be confirmed. Apologists for the black establishment have suggested that this was the result of ignorance.

They maintain that "Thomas expressed views . . . rejected by the great majority of blacks."

> The fact that many blacks, particularly in the South, appeared to favor Thomas' confirmation doesn't suggest otherwise. As Roger Wilkins has pointed out, typically these supporters either did not fully appreciate how much Thomas' views diverged from their own or else they supported him in spite of his views out of an "instinctive reaction" to support one of their own.[1]

There is a typically patronizing illogic to the notion that black Americans were incapable of making a reasonable judgment about a man who, for several weeks, became one of the most watched and talked about people in America. It's far more likely that many people in the black-American community were repulsed by the sight of their supposed leaders eagerly joining the mob which sought to tear down a man who was so obviously one of their own. Thomas had an up-from-poverty background with which most black Americans instinctively identify. When he spoke about the importance of his grandfather's influence and example, when he dared to suggest that his own self-discipline and hard work had something to do with his success in life, they sensed in him the same spirit that has motivated blacks throughout American history. They saw him as a fitting representative of black-America's character and its characteristic values.

In the eyes of the black establishment, this background was irrelevant. Thomas may have been one of us, but he wasn't one of them. His insistence on taking some share of the credit for his own advancement especially offended them. In their view, black Americans today owe any achievements in their lives to affirmative-action programs, the very programs which, as a conservative black, they said Thomas opposed. Ironically, in the effort to damn Thomas as an ingrate biting the hand that feeds him, the leadership revealed the posture they think most appropriate for black Americans: on our knees thanking "massah gubmint" for benefits and favors received. Thomas supposed opposition to affirmative action wasn't what chiefly motivated the black establishment to oppose him. His main offense was simply that he never parroted the agenda of the union bureaucrats and left-liberal Democrats who seem to control the elite voices that are supposed to speak for black Americans. Unlike the union bureaucrats, he apparently believes that there are limits to what government can or should do, even in the name of social progress. Unlike the left-liberal Democrats, he thinks that some traditional social and sexual mores should be preserved. In many respects, Thomas simply stands for the basic values of family, faith, and self-improvement that form the bedrock of black-American character.

Despite this fact, the established black leaders admitted no kinship with Thomas. His adherence to fundamental values of the black community meant nothing to them, since in their eyes, the black community is not based on shared values, but only on adherence to a certain set of political views. Since the triumphant first wave of the Civil Rights movement, a dominant collective personality has emerged among establishment black leaders. It means that for the most part, these leaders are statists, they are leftists, and they are intensely partisan Democrats. Thus, where economic policies are concerned, they have an almost religious faith in government action. They consider themselves the natural allies of any who seek a radical transformation of social and sexual mores of the country. They regard any deviation from strict allegiance to the Democratic party as practically a crime against black humanity.

The black establishment's faith in government action was, in part, the result of habits of mind formed during the Civil Rights movement. Federal court actions and civil rights legislation of the 1960s (e.g., the Voting Rights Act of 1965; the Fair Housing laws; court-ordered desegregation efforts) ended the system of state-sponsored racial segregation and discrimination in the United

States. Naturally, these great civil rights victories appeared to vindicate the strategy used to produce them. On the one hand, the work of the NAACP Legal Defense Fund led to battles and victories in the federal court system that overthrew segregation in education. On the other hand, direct nonviolent action, such as boycotts, marches, freedom rides, and sit-ins, created crisis situations that focused national attention on the issue of racial injustice, and developed pressure for corrective action from the federal government. The key lay in the mobilization of national power against abuses at state and local levels. The first March on Washington in 1963 marked the stirring culmination of this strategy. It was a dramatic demonstration of the political clout of an emerging national consensus favoring racial reform.

For decades after Emancipation, the perceptions created by the Civil War era determined black America's views and allegiances. Similarly, the epic civil rights battles of the 1960s did much to define the basic views and allegiances of black America in the decades that followed. Federal intervention was the key to the major civil rights advances; hence, the perception that centralized federal power is good. State and local governments were the rallying points for resistance to desegregation; therefore, decentralized state and local power is suspect. Claims of private prerogative and choice were used to defend discriminatory practices; therefore, an unregulated private sector is dangerous. Liberal Democrats and union bureaucrats proved to be major allies in civil rights victories; in the black political dictionary, therefore, they are defined as friends. Conservative Republicans joined southern Democrats to fight against them, so they are defined as enemies.

Given the importance and intensity of the issues at stake for the black community, it's not surprising that black Americans made their judgments about people and institutions in American society based on a sense of who stood where on the issue of racial justice. But what began as a judgment about issues has become over time a dogmatic assumption, much like the unthinking black allegiance to the Republican party in the half-century after Reconstruction. Today's deeply black establishment relies on it to maintain its leadership position. In support of their unswerving partisanship, they have developed a mythology meant to encourage the belief that in order to be authentically black, every African American must share their government-obsessed left-wing ideology.

According to this mythology, the justification for black America's automatic allegiance to liberal Democratic politicians and programs dates back to the New Deal era. Black liberals often cite New Deal employment and welfare programs as the models for what needs to be done to address economic ills in the black community today. Given this faith in New Deal kind of solutions, one would assume that the New Deal produced extraordinary benefits for the black community. In fact, the opposite is closer to the truth. During the 1930s, most blacks still lived in the South. White southerners were the keystone of the Democratic Party's chances in presidential elections. Once elected, Roosevelt needed the support of white southerners in order to secure passage of his administration's ambitious legislative agenda.[2] Therefore, despite pressure from civil rights organizations throughout the New Deal era, the Roosevelt administration was unwilling to push for federal legislation against the lynchings and racial violence that continually claimed black victims. FDR also allowed racist southern whites to control local administration of New Deal programs.[3] Their ascendancy virtually excluded blacks from equitable participation in most of them.

> Despite an official policy of nondiscrimination, relief administration was in the hands of state and local officials, whose attitudes and prejudices governed the treatment of blacks. Some people in Washington agreed with them. Lorena Hickok, who toured the country for Harry Hopkins, had considerable sympathy for the point of view of the local administrators. Her observations in the South and West convinced her of the merits of a double standard which would permit

them to apply racial classifications in the distribution of relief. Given such views, it was not surprising to find, especially in the South, that discrimination in relief administration was more often the rule than the exception.[4]

New Deal agricultural programs, for instance, favored white farmers at the expense of blacks. As a result, tens of thousands of black farmers were squeezed out.

Nearly two million black people worked in agriculture in 1930; of those, roughly 306,000 were tenant farmers and 393,000 were sharecroppers. The AAA [Agricultural Adjustment Administration] was single handedly responsible for a drastic curtailment in their numbers—over the decade of the 1930s, the number of black tenants was cut by nearly a third and the number of croppers by just under a quarter. By comparison, the number of white tenants actually grew between 1930 and 1935, but then leveled off by 1940 to a number virtually identical to that of 1930. The number of white sharecroppers, however, fell by 37 percent.[5]

Racial bias limited black access to self-reliance-oriented public-works projects, like the Civilian Conservation Corps (CCC).[6] On the other hand, blacks swelled the roles of the New Deal emergency relief programs because they were the only ones to which they had relatively equitable access.[7] The racial discrimination that marred the administration of New Deal programs would have continued unabated during the war years but for continual pressure from people like A. Philip Randolph, the principal leader of organized black labor. He successfully spearheaded a black coalition that threatened to organize thousands of blacks in a March on Washington unless the Roosevelt administration took steps to limit racial bias in the war effort.[8]

Many blacks at the time were well aware of the New Deal's

shortcomings. Stories and complaints about the racist administration of New Deal programs appeared frequently in the black press. Black commentators pointed to the demoralizing effects New Deal welfare programs were having on the moral infrastructure of the black community.

Black leaders worried that the New Deal would leave the race in worse straits than before. Francis E. Rivers, a Republican lawyer in Harlem, warned of the creation of a permanent class of black reliefers, no longer employable in private industry. William Lloyd Imes, a Harlem minister, expressed concern that "the Negro is rapidly having his status as an underprivileged and last-to-be-thought-of man absolutely crystallized in Federal practice." John P. Davis, executive secretary of the Joint Committee on National Recovery, sounded similar notes in his public speeches. "The total effect of the government's social experiments" had been "to plan for permanent poverty."[9]

Excluded from the programs that might have put them on the road to steady work and self-reliance, many blacks instead were herded toward the welfare trough of dead-end dependency.

Today, black liberals routinely speak of the New Deal as if it marked a major advance for black Americans. In fact, it did nothing of the kind. The discriminatory administration of New Deal programs harmed many blacks economically, and pushed them in directions that weakened the moral fiber of the black community. As one of A. Philip Randolph's biographers put it, "For the majority of black Americans, the New Deal had turned out to be a revolution only in their expectations."[10] The white planners who devised the New Deal's programs were not thinking about blacks, and did not much care what happened to them. Consider, for example, the Social Security program.

As it finally emerged, the Social Security program excluded agricultural and domestic employees from its provisions for unemployment compensation and old-age insurance. This exclusion, the NAACP's legal counsel asserted, was a "direct blow at Negro workers," for two thirds of gainfully employed blacks worked in precisely those . . . occupations.[11]

Similarly, the efforts of the National Recovery Administration (NRA) to raise labor standards largely bypassed blacks since they did not apply to areas where blacks tended to work (i.e., agricultural and domestic employment). Ironically, in other sectors, NRA-enforced wage rates hastened black bankruptcies and led to thousands of blacks being displaced by white employees.[12]

The New Deal's inequitable treatment of blacks arose from Roosevelt's unwillingness to challenge the racist attitudes that prevailed in America at the time, particularly in the South. Yet FDR achieved enormous popularity in the black community. This came in part from symbolic gestures of racial tolerance from FDR, and especially from his wife, Eleanor.[13] It also reflected the fact that, though rampant discrimination continued in practice, FDR's declared policy was to include all needy Americans. Since racist exclusion and economic deprivation had become the norm, most blacks saw any acknowledgment of their participation, albeit only in the nation's hardships, as an improvement. Finally, black support for FDR reflected the severity of the economic crisis blacks, like many other Americans, faced at the time. Given the grim hardship and economic insecurity they were experiencing, many felt deeply grateful even for an unequal share in government-sponsored relief efforts. At least it gave them a chance to survive.[14]

Among blacks, Roosevelt also benefited from the fact that his Republican opponents had grown so complacent and uncaring about black support. Sixty years after the end of the Civil War, Republicans could still rely on the memory of Lincoln and Emancipation to secure automatic black backing in those relatively few areas of the country where black votes mattered.[15] This was true despite the fact that Republicans had done little to prevent the virtual elimination of blacks from voters' rolls throughout the South. Indeed, even in the North, most Republicans had dropped all pretense of disagreeing with the racist southern Democrats who engineered black political disenfranchisement and Jim Crow segregation in the southern states. After years of unswerving black loyalty, Republicans ceased to feel any need to take the black community's situation seriously. In the election of 1932, Herbert Hoover's poor record on issues affecting black America accurately symbolized the general Republican indifference toward blacks.[16]

Republican neglect offered white Democrats an effective opportunity to break the Republican monopoly on the allegiance of black voters. In states like Roosevelt's home base, New York, black votes could make an important contribution to the margin of victory in state and local races as well as the quadrennial contest for presidential electoral votes. Though the black community remained loyally Republican in 1932 when FDR was first elected, in the election of 1936, Roosevelt managed to win a solid majority of black votes. He did so without losing the racist white southerners or rank-and-file union members who were the core of the Democrats' national electoral base. Subsistence relief programs won the gratitude of the economically desperate black masses. Token participation in the New Deal's administrative structures addressed the ambitions of more elite blacks. Thus Roosevelt was able to use federal assistance and patronage to win black goodwill while leaving the power and exclusionary racial policies of state and local Democratic chieftains undisturbed.

The political reality imposed on blacks by New Deal politics set the pattern for decades to come. Other ethnic groups (e.g., Irish, Italians) were gradually able to develop local political power bases as their voting power reached sufficient strength. But especially in the South, where their numerical strength was concentrated, blacks were excluded from participation.[17] Therefore, they could not build local power bases. They could not use their local numerical strength to bargain their way into positions of greater influence at the state and national levels. The New Deal did nothing to challenge this exclusion.

Where African Americans are concerned, the calculating reality of FDR's use of federal power runs counter to the benign view of it enforced as sacred dogma by the ideological watchdogs of the black liberal establishment. When the federal government finally took on a critical role in the success of the struggle for black civil rights, it was not because New Deal liberalism encouraged such a role. In fact, the Democratic party's national strength was based on a coalition between white racists and their black victims. It protected the powerful southern bigots who maintained Jim Crow institutions in the old Confederacy. It also included major unions whose locals often insisted on practicing stubborn discrimination against blacks in the industrial areas of the North. Until the Civil Rights movement forced the situation in the late fifties, New Deal coalition politics did little to address the fundamental issues of segregation and discrimination. In the South, the coalition challenged neither the legal structures of racial segregation nor the political power structure that supported it. In the North, it left undisturbed the local political coalitions that abetted the practice of racial discrimination. Though recognized within the coalition as spokesmen for their race, black leaders were excluded from the competition for positions of leadership in the community at large. Thus the black community could never take its turn in the major seats of local political power. While successfully portraying itself as progressive in rhetoric and image, FDR's Democratic coalition helped to preserve the racist status quo.

Blacks played a subordinate, passive role in the New Deal coalition. They would have done so indefinitely but for their own agitation against the system of racial oppression. Change came about because blacks themselves asserted, in political form, the traditional black values of self-help and self-reliance. In the late 1950s, when blacks began to organize effectively against Jim Crow racism and discrimination, their assertiveness posed a major threat to the viability of New Deal political arrangements. If Democratic party leaders gave in to the demand for racial equality, southern whites might desert the Democratic banner. If they took steps to remove obstacles to black participation in major job sectors, rank-and-file union members might lose their enthusiasm for the Democratic ticket. If they supported a more equal black participation in local political power and influence, local politicians might sabotage the party's chances for federal office. Yet if the Democrats failed to respond to black civil rights demands, they might create an opportunity for Republicans to recapture black support.

Though in our day liberalism recommends itself to black Americans as a compassionate response to the problems of poverty and injustice, it was also a response to the political dangers posed by the determined independence black America displayed during the early years of the Civil Rights movement. Liberal white power holders responded out of sympathy, but also out of fear. They feared the civil disturbances that erupted when growing expectations led blacks to vent their resentment and frustration through violence. They feared the moral scars that would result if the white community resisted all change, and responded to violence with excessive force. And like all wielders of power, they simply feared the existence of forces over which they had no certain influence or control.

The Democrats had to find a way of dealing with these dilemmas that would keep their unnatural coalition from imploding. The first stage of their response culminated in the passage of the 1964 Civil Rights Act which committed federal power to an effort to secure basic political participation for southern blacks by dismantling the structures of political disenfranchisement at state and local levels. Here, the political calculation was simple. As a result of the great migration, there were many more black voters in states outside the South. Securing a solid black vote in northern urban areas could therefore offset the loss of solid white support in the South. It quickly became clear, though, that legislative actions would not be enough. Some black leaders, such as A. Philip Randolph and Bayard Rustin, had always insisted that removal of the legal structures of discrimination had to be accompanied by efforts to address the economic and political consequences of decades of racial discrimination. In the mid-sixties, these economic and political concerns moved to the top of the black agenda. Influenced by such Third World intellectuals as Frantz Fanon, young black radicals produced angry leftist critiques lambasting the allegedly inherent racism of America's capitalist society. Martin Luther King's stirring rhetoric of racial justice and reform gave way to the more strident rhetoric of "Black Power." Some groups, such as the Black Panthers, espoused and tried to implement violent revolutionary approaches. Large-scale rioting in black urban ghettos suggested that this angry frustration wasn't confined to a few student radicals.

Black leaders wrestled with the challenge of developing strategies and approaches that would effectively address these feelings and the economic bondage from which they sprang. Their efforts brought them into conflict with other important elements of the Democratic coalition at the local level. The result: awkward confrontations like Martin Luther King's skirmishes with Mayor Richard Daley in Chicago.[18] It became evident that southern whites were not the only ones whose local power monopolies would be broken by black demands for justice. These demands implied a restructuring of power and a redistribution of scarce resources at the grassroots level, in order to accommodate black claims to full participation. Blacks were demanding equal access to decent schools, jobs, housing, and community services, including health care and law enforcement. This meant that other groups in the community might have to surrender past advantages or move more slowly up the ladder of economic and political status. Local Democratic chieftains as well as union bosses and other civic leaders had to find some way of managing the political strains this restructuring implied.

One answer to this challenge lay in shifting demographic patterns. These patterns reflected white flight into the suburbs, away from the need for political accommodation with emerging black majorities (or decisive pluralities) in urban centers. Given enough time, this shift would reduce the political dangers of racial friction. In the interim, Great Society liberalism offered local Democratic leaders a way to manage black demands. In a slightly altered disguise, it repeated the successful formula of the New Deal. Instead of being compensated for their political support with reciprocal access to state and local seats of power, blacks received access to an array of new federal programs and benefits.[19] This postponed their ascendancy in those localities where their numbers promised decisive political influence. In most cases, blacks finally gained control of such urban centers only to find that their economic base was no longer self-sufficient. By the time blacks reached city hall, the urban centers they now led could barely stave off bankruptcy, even with large doses of state and federal funds.

The Los Angeles riots of 1992 stirred renewed debate over the legacy of the Great Society programs. For black Americans, the programs certainly helped a certain number of individuals. But they left the black community weaker than ever. Despite early rhetoric about community participation and development (the famous requirement for "maximum feasible participation" by people in target communities), Great Society programs ended up putting control of the lives and affairs of poor urban blacks firmly in the hands of the bureaucracy. This was not an accident, but a conscious choice, made to prevent the programs from undermining local networks of power.

Less than a year after OEO [Office of Economic Opportunity] was established, James Rowe, a former Roosevelt aide and Johnson friend, was warning the President that the local community action agency was staging protests against Democratic leaders in the District of Columbia. Johnson was emphatic; in a handwritten note to Bill Moyers he demanded, "For God's sake get on top of this and stop it at once. . . ." After Mayoral complaints about CAP [Community Action Program] had intensified during the summer of 1965, Budget Director Charles Schultze told the President that the "maximum feasible participation" requirement was receiving the wrong kind of emphasis. Instead of giving the poor jobs, getting them to volunteer, and keeping them informed about the progress of programs, CAP was focusing on putting the poor onto local poverty boards, holding elections and organizing the poor. The chief executive approved Schultze's suggestion that OEO be instructed to get CAP out of the business of setting up "competing political groups."[20]

The community action agencies were by no means exclusively for black Americans. However, as Moynihan observed in his essay on the community action effort, "It would appear that by and large, in large cities, community action came to be primarily associated with the cause of Negro betterment."[21] Unfortunately, the dangled carrot of participation proved to be a treacherous pitfall. In the social-science view of the black community, the real institutions of community self-government—the churches—were practically invisible. As a result, Great Society social engineers moved in to reinvent them. In this effort, radical left-wing notions of mass mobilization through anger and disaffection predominated. Instead of looking for and working with representatives of the decent, churchgoing, "poor but proud" black working class, they sought out elements of the community who could most easily arouse and symbolize disaffection. Starting from a false premise, they could not but reach a bad conclusion.

Over and again [sic], the attempt by official and quasi-official agencies (such as the Ford Foundation) to organize poor communities led first to the radicalization of the middle-class persons who began the effort; next to a certain amount of stirring among the poor . . . next to retaliation from the larger white community; whereupon it would emerge that the community action agency, which had talked so much, been so much in the headlines, promised so much in the way of change in the fundamentals of things, was powerless. A creature of a Washington bureaucracy, subject to discontinuation without notice.[22]

With greater truth than perhaps he intends, Moynihan goes on to sum up the situation of blacks challenging the local power structures in their communities:

Decision-making in Syracuse is as diffuse a process as in most medium American cities, yet to a pronounced degree events there are influenced by a fairly small number of men in banks and law firms whose names are not generally known, who do not run for Congress, who do not run for mayor. . . . They were and remain the tough power brokers of an American city, and they can outwait a black "agent provocateur" anytime if that individual is dependent on the House of Representatives and the General Accounting Office to stay in business.[23]

Once it became clear that black aspirations went beyond more benefits, and even beyond greater acceptance and integration, the position that Moynihan ascribes to the black *agent provocateur* was in fact the position, within the New Deal coalition, of the black community as a whole. The community made provocative demands for an equitable share of power. On the whole, the response of the Democratic party's national power brokers was much like the one Moynihan describes at the local level. They distracted the black community's pursuit of power with the offer of positions and programs that live or die by federal determinations. When black leaders accepted the offer, the national power brokers, too, had only to wait them out, secure in the knowledge that they could make or break this illusion of progress anytime they pleased.

The radicalization of the community action effort provided the ideal excuse to stigmatize as radical and communist-inspired black demands for a real share of local political power. The agents fomenting this radicalism were planted and raised in the community by federal bureaucrats, before being discovered there by an outraged public. Still, they could then be used to suggest (as Moynihan quietly does in his essay) that the poor (meaning, in most cases, black Americans) aren't ready for power and can't be trusted to handle it safely.

During the years of forced separation and exclusion from American politics, the black community had developed its own church-based institutions of community self-government. But the liberal planners and social engineers never bothered seriously to investigate their potential. They were blinded by the assumptions of their social-science methodology, and in many cases, their decidedly leftist (and therefore antireligious) predisposition. So in the early days of the liberal response to the black revolt, though the core institutions of the black community had never actually been mobilized or involved, the community action concept was discredited, and with it, the notion of local black political empowerment. Former Speaker of the House Tip O'Neill used to say that in America "all politics is local politics." The foundation of real political clout is the power position people achieve at the grassroots level, and this means first of all their ability to control their own affairs. Liberalism induced blacks to focus their energies instead on the federal level. Black issues were automatically redefined as national issues, requiring federal action, but also, therefore, federal administration and oversight. Exaggerated talk about "black power" gave way to the reality of increased government power in and over the lives of the black poor. Indeed, in the lexicon of liberal orthodoxy, the expansion of government power became synonymous with black advancement.

Though clothed in the rhetoric of compassion and social concern, New Deal and Great Society liberalism proved in the end to be a tough-minded strategy for dealing with black America's revolt against the unjust racial regime in America. It created concepts and institutions that captured and redirected the ambition of the educated elite, the individuals whose energy provided the articulate voice and leadership for the revolt. Many of the leaders of the black liberal establishment today came up through the system created for this purpose. They are people like Marion Barry in Washington, D.C., who parlayed opportunities in or related to the government-based antipoverty structure into political machines that allowed them to achieve a dominant position within the black community. But unlike the ethnic urban political machines of America's not-too-distant past, these political bases were not built on the real bargaining position of the black community in relation to other groups at the local level. They relied instead on federal programs, federal money, federal power. Thus, the position of these leaders depends on outcomes at the federal level. They are not dependent on the black community for their positions. Indeed, the opposite is true: They achieve personal power by inducing people in the community to rely on them for access to government patronage and benefits. Therefore, these leaders don't represent the strength of the black community; they represent its weakness, dependency, and continued political subjugation.

By getting them to establish their personal power bases at the federal level, Great Society liberalism hindered black leaders from developing the black community's local strength into an effective and powerful brokerage position. Instead of emerging gradually as local power brokers, black leaders sunk ever more deeply into the quagmire of perpetual supplication. Power remained something to which the community appealed, rather than something it fashioned, wielded, and understood. This is symbolized by the fact that black political demands focused so much on the level of government furthest from the actual influence and control of the people.

Though it did not serve the political interest of the black community as a whole, the federalization of the black agenda offered important advantages to some elements of the black elite. As long as they play their role as shills for ineffective, but politically salient, national programs, they can expect rich rewards from the white power holders whose local power bases they help to maintain. For the black masses, however, particularly in urban areas, the nationalization of black politics means the perpetuation of their status as effectively disenfranchised, second-class citizens. Federally-funded programs, particularly those aimed at training people for real jobs, may offer a limited number of people an avenue to permanent self-improvement. However, the lion's share of the federal government's social-welfare spending is devoted to subsistence programs offering stipends and subsidies on terms that foster permanent psychological and material dependency. Beyond subsistence transfer payments, the main product of federal social welfare spending is government jobs,[24] either through direct employment or through contracts to provide services. The subsistence programs provide patronage to enthrall the poor black masses, while government jobs provide patronage to embroil and manipulate more elite blacks. Together they are the "bread and circuses" that help to keep black Americans passively in the sway of the liberal empire.

Jesse Jackson's career illustrates the liberal ideology's power over the black leadership. In order to pursue his presidential ambitions within the Democratic coalition, he had to conform to the liberal paradigm that dominates national black leadership. But in his early career Jackson did not proceed on the assumption that, for blacks, all politics is national politics.[25] Jackson began by organizing the Chicago black community to put pressure on private-sector enterprises for a larger role in the private sector. He also preached the value of discipline, hard work, and responsibility (including sexual responsibility and the importance of marriage) to teens and other young blacks. This was in line with the traditional values of the community. It was also in line with the doctrine of improvement through economic development preached by Booker T. Washington, and put into practice at an everyday level by the majority of black Americans. Jackson's economic agenda combined two seemingly disparate principles: The black community must organize, and develop its own economic and moral resources; but blacks must also have access to jobs, capital, and ownership in the economy at large. He pursued self-reliance, but not isolation; group solidarity, but not separation or withdrawal from the society at large. This combination allowed Jackson to be militant while staying well within the boundaries of mainstream society. And it worked.

Using the leverage of the black community's purchasing power (through the threat and use of boycotts), Jackson induced local businesses to employ more blacks. Similar methods contributed to successful negotiations with large national brands (e.g., Coca-Cola, Heublein, 7UP) for more black distributorships and even advertising in black-owned media outlets. Jackson's tactics brought him into conflict with local power structures, including, of course, the black leaders who had made their position and their peace with the Daley-dominated Chicago Democratic machine. But it also allowed him to put effective pressure on other local elements to improve the relative power share of the black community.

The notoriety Jackson earned with his successes created the opportunity for him to bid for preeminence as the national spokesman for America's blacks. This was the role he had always sought. His efforts in Chicago were only a stepping stone toward this role. He had no desire to resist the temptation. Unfortunately, this required a transformation. He had to conform to the requirements of the collective personality of national black leadership. Why? In order to develop a national base within the Democratic party. Jackson abandoned the strategy of organizing black people to push more effectively into the private sector, and into the local power structure. Instead of helping others around the country to apply the tactics he used so successfully in Chicago, Jackson abandoned the principle on which it was based. As a national leader, Jackson has become a shill for the usual establishment agenda—more government programs, more federal spending. He abandoned the agenda of local development and power-sharing.

He has also adopted the compulsory agenda of the left wing of the Democratic party on issues affecting the nation's mores. Abortion is a case in point. The early Jackson, in line with values and traditions of black America's deep religious faith, opposed abortion. He argued sincerely and cogently that, as a child from a disadvantaged background (as he portrayed it), he himself would have been aborted. He saw the implied denigration in the position that children who will be born into poverty or oppression should never see the light of day. He also understood the genocidal implications of this position for the black community. Once he decided to bid for national leadership, however, he changed his position on abortion to conform with the requirements of leftist ideologues who seem to dictate the social values of national black leadership.

The Jesse Jackson of Chicago PUSH and the campaigns to achieve economic penetration for blacks was all about black pride and achievement. The Jesse Jackson of national presidential politics has been all about black helplessness. One saw blacks as externally repressed but internally capable; the other sees blacks as essentially helpless victims. For one, the key to black advancement was local empowerment, meaning the achievement of a greater share of political and economic assets at the local level. For the other, the key is government programs, meaning more control in the hands of government bureaucrats. The early Jackson's actions and principles reflected his authentic involvement with the black community at the grassroots level. The later Jackson is a man refashioned to suit the assumptions of the black role in the Democratic coalition.

Jackson's transformation tells us a great deal about the nature of the established national leadership of the black community. Though enshrined by the media as spokesmen for the black community, their agenda is more horizontal than vertical; that is, it reflects what they must do to maintain good relations with their elite white counterparts in the Democratic coalition, not what they should do to improve the economic and political power position of the black community.

For example, the Congressional Black Caucus, which supposedly reflects the mainstream opinion of the black community, votes and speaks unanimously in favor of the so-called pro-choice position. All black Congressional representatives are on record as supporters of the Freedom of Choice Act,[26] which would, in effect, impose unrestricted abortion-on-demand even on those states that presently have more restrictive legislation (parental notification, late-term restrictions, and so forth). Yet polls have consistently shown strong antiabortion feeling in the black community, and overwhelming support for at least some restrictions.[27] Abortions also have a disproportionately damaging effect on the black population. Though blacks constitute only 12 percent of the overall population, black women account for nearly a third of the abortions performed annually. Two black babies are being aborted for every three born.

All this means that in recent years, abortion has removed nearly half-a-million blacks from the population each year. A pogrom that caused that many deaths in any ethnic or racial population would surely be considered genocidal. Despite this disproportionate impact, black leaders stridently advance the argument that poor women need access to abortion to prevent the tragedy of children being born into poverty. Of course, since most black people in American history were poor and oppressed, this would have been an argument for preventing most black births at any given time in the past. In fact, it was used as such. In line with her slogan, "More from the fit, less from the unfit," Margaret Sanger, the founder of the Planned Parenthood organization, advocated an effort to prevent black births, the so-called "Negro Project." As part of this project, she and her associates intended to

> hire three or four colored ministers, preferably with social-service backgrounds, and with engaging personalities. The most successful educational approach to the Negro is through a religious appeal. And we do not want word to go out that we want to exterminate the Negro population, and the minister is the man who can straighten out that idea if it ever occurs to any of their more rebellious members.[28]

Though she didn't want word to get out, Sanger associated openly with rabid racist and antisemitic advocates of white racial purity like Lothrop Stoddard[29] and C. C. Little, cofounders of the American Birth Control League.

Today, Margaret Sanger's idea of those "unfit" to be born has become the notion of the "unwanted" births, with the children of poor (and even not so poor) black women automatically placed in the unwanted category. Given that the abortion-rights movement has such racist antecedents, and given its disproportionately destructive impact on the black population, it makes sense for it to be viewed in the black community with suspicion, if not hostility. Yet the established black leaders are unanimous and even strident in their support of abortion rights. In this they do not seek to represent the black community's values (which are decidedly anti-abortion), but to change them in order to conform with the dictates of "politically correct" liberal orthodoxy.

In the same manner, following the lead of the highly organized public-education bureaucrats, black leaders have spoken out against efforts to institute school-choice programs that would allow parents to decide how at least part of the public funds available for education would be spent. Using vouchers or some other form of direct support, parents could authorize public expenditures up to a given limit, at whatever school they decide best serves the educational needs of their children. For poor blacks in particular, these programs could offer a path to greater influence over unresponsive public-school systems, or a way to finance alternatives when they are dissatisfied with the public schools' performance. Such alternatives are only available today to people with substantial incomes, or to others willing to make inordinate sacrifices. In addition, teachers and others with innovative ideas for reaching hard-to-teach children in poor urban areas could set up alternative schools, knowing that even in those poor areas parents attracted by their promise or success could command a chunk of the resources now under the exclusive control of the public-education bureaucrats. At the grassroots level in some parts of the country, blacks have been in the forefront of efforts to establish school-choice programs. Yet the established black leaders continue to toe the line drawn by the National Education Association and its allies.

Similar situations exist on a host of issues, from moral controversies like gay rights, to social issues like gun control; from economic questions, like the so-called striker-replacement legislation,[30] to complex issues like Congressional approval of the North American Free Trade Agreement. The stances adopted by established black leaders on such issues may be right, they may be wrong. But in many instances, from the vantage point of black America's interests, a good case can be made on the other side. At the very least, this would suggest that the leadership ought to remain open-minded on these issues, respecting and even encouraging discussion, debate, and a diversity of viewpoints in the black community. Positions within the black community on such issues ought to depend on how black people in different states and communities see their interests being affected. What's helpful in one place may not be suitable in another. Instead, the leadership has taken emphatic stands in line with positions demanded by their partners in the national Democratic coalition. They arguably sacrifice the real interests of local black communities in order to sustain their relations with their national coalition partners. In return, they continue to be paid in the coinage of federal spending programs that empower bureaucracies and the black elite while leaving blacks in communities and neighborhoods at the grassroots level more powerless and manipulated than ever.

Of course, the mere fact of powerlessness isn't enough to account for the heightened institutional crisis in the black community today. Black Americans were always relatively powerless, but their strong moral identity gave them the wherewithal to sustain their basic social institutions. Material deprivation failed to degrade black Americans in the past, because they resisted the notion that their material circumstances determined their worth or potential as human beings. But the materialism of modern social science and social engineering shouldered aside a black-American value system that gave primacy to morality and spirituality. Large-scale reliance on the welfare system obscured the community's traditional belief in hard work, self-reliance, and self-improvement as the keys to survival and progress. Most important, domination by the impersonal structures of the bureaucratic state undermined or pushed aside black America's traditional reliance on family and church as the roots of personality and security. When they accepted the deal that underlies black participation in the liberal coalition, black leadership abandoned the foundations of black America's moral identity, which were, in fact, the foundations of our survival.

Elijah rock, shout! shout!
Elijah rock, comin' up Lord.
The Devil is a liar and a conjure, too,
If you don't watch out, he'll conjure you!

Chapter 7

NOT

BY

BREAD

ALONE

During the Civil Rights movement, black Americans clearly demonstrated the strength of character forged by our history. Ironically, in its aftermath, welfare-state liberalism spawned programs and institutions that encouraged many blacks who depended on them to lose touch with this heritage, to lose faith in themselves, and to believe those fraternal twins—racism and economic disadvantage—mean they can accomplish nothing on their own. As one analyst puts it, "The desire to work succumbs to defeatism" and "a sheer disbelief that one ever could work on one's own."[1] During the Great Society era, this psychology of defeat and dependency gradually subverted the concepts of self-discipline, self-improvement, and moral autonomy that characterized the black American tradition. The relatively poor black masses were led to believe that their betterment depended more upon government action and largesse than upon their own efforts.

It's important to note here that I am not arguing that the liberal welfare state simply created problems that didn't already exist. Tendencies toward moral dissolution certainly existed in the black community, as they do in every community. But so did strong countervailing tendencies, particularly represented within black churches. Until the imposition of the welfare-state system, these countervailing positive forces were more than holding their own in the battle for moral stability within the community. The liberal welfare state entered the picture like a large new army thrown into the fray on the side of moral dissolution. Rather than working with and reenforcing the moralizing influences and institutions within the community, it gave aid and comfort to its antimoral tendencies.

Consider, for example, the problem of premarital sexual activity and illegitimacy. From slavery times until today, there has been a high incidence of these problems in the black community. This was, at least partly, the legacy of a slave system that prized black sexual activity for breeding purposes, devoid of any moral purpose or intention; and which exposed black women, in particular, to violation and exploitation by white males who were legally forbidden to marry them. It may also owe something to an African tradition in which the regulation of sexual behavior is primarily a social rather than ethical imperative.[2] However, both in traditional African systems,[3] and in the system that evolved in the black-American context, marriage and family remained the ultimate focus, goal, and context of sexual behavior. Young black men and women might play around for a while, but it was understood that they had to marry and settle down in order to be accepted as adults within decent society. Among blacks in the prewelfare state era, there probably wasn't less sexual activity than today, but there was greater pressure to marry.[4] The welfare-state system disrupted this social pattern by offering a source of economic and social support for irresponsible behavior, without any corresponding pressure to normalize the behavior. When young people had to rely on family or church networks for support, they eventually encountered and had to respond to such pressure, or risk being cut off from the community's support network.

The availability of state support eliminated the need to accommodate this moralizing influence. In effect, it empowered immorality while undermining the moral influence of the community's basic institutions—the extended family and the church. As we have seen, black churches, in particular, had been the vital focus of energy, leadership, and inspiration for the community. But the secularism encouraged by the welfare-state mentality lured the black poor away from their practical dependence upon churches and the network of internal institutions they represent. Initially, government-based "community action programs" sucked in the autonomous structures of black community activism. When those programs faded, the naked reality of bureaucratic domination took hold. Black churches, as well as other organizing and moralizing institutions within the community, were relegated to the role of theaters of emotional catharsis—much the same role the enslavers wanted them to play during slavery.

Of course, the subsidies of the welfare state weren't the only factors undermining the position of these institutions. The 1960s saw the beginning of a general retreat from traditional mores throughout American society, spurred by the emergence of a popular culture that emphasized acquisitive materialism and selfish hedonism. Self-fulfillment became the definition of happiness, with sexual pleasure and money (or the things money can buy) as the main barometers of its attainment. The driving force behind this culture wasn't ideological, but economic. In the decades after World War II, mass consumption became the engine of economic expansion. The mass communications media provided the means to stimulate consumption on the scale required. But in order to produce the desired effect, the message conveyed by the media had to break down the moral and psychological inhibitions on consumption.

Traditional mores encouraged people to feel that self-indulgence should be limited by a sense of responsibility, obligation, or moral discipline. In the context of a strong ethic of marriage and family, for example, the desire to be "sexy" was more or less confined to the youthful years before marriage and parenthood. The need for clothes or other possessions assumed to attract the opposite sex also decreased significantly once one found a dependable marriage partner. Maturity implied above all the ability to discipline and control one's desires, to reduce or eliminate personal needs that complicated or interfered with the effort to meet one's responsibilities to family and community. This was especially true for working people, whose livelihood often depended on their ability to put aside self-indulgent temptations.

The mass-consumption economy made such notions seem obsolete and counterproductive. Where consumption is the law and the prophets, self-discipline is heresy. More is always better. Since maturity places limits on the desire for more, maturity is out. Adolescence comes into its own. The best consumers are perpetual teenagers, people for whom personal desires are fresh and mysterious, and who, therefore, find it hard to accept having any limits placed upon them. They are always wanting and needing what the market has to offer. Of course, in the old days, adolescents were mostly assumed to be dependent upon their more mature elders for the money they needed to finance their consumption. But to achieve a mass base of consumption, the link between work and maturity had to be broken. The mass-consumption economy needs full-fledged earners whose desires remain untrammeled by any limiting sense of obligation to others. It thrives on people who acquire the skills to earn, but who remain emotionally single and self-centered. It needs adults who are adolescents with a paycheck. This concept of adulthood has come to dominate the mass media, in advertising as well as in entertainment. Television shows, music videos, movies, and pop-culture magazines glorify the successful consumer, the man or woman who "has it all." By implication, they denigrate people of limited means or self-limited desires, who lack the resources or the ambition to be successful in this way.

Thus, at the same time the expanding welfare state pulled aside the influence of the key moral institutions in the black community, unbridled sensualism and materialism emerged as the basis of popular culture in our society at large. What's more, a certain stereotype of black Americans played an important role in the triumph of this popular culture. In the racist mythology, blacks were portrayed as supremely sensual and sexually uninhibited. In fact, of course, most blacks were no more uninhibited than most whites. Thanks to the dominant church-based culture of the black community, they may even have been less so, especially where unusual sexual practices are concerned. But beside the dominant church-based culture of the black community, a secular subculture thrived, whose music and mores seemed to justify the stereotype. First in New Orleans, then in Harlem and on Chicago's South Side, this culture thrived. Its high priests were the musicians and singers who translated the blend of rhythm and melody that characterized black church music to a secular setting, where sensual passion and fatalistic cynicism replaced spirituality and dogged faith. Blues, jazz, and eventually rock and roll music either emerged from or were deeply influenced by this secular black culture.

In the bars, clubs, and honky-tonks where black music held sway, racial integration had a long history. As the movement against overt racial segregation came to a head in the sixties, the emerging popular culture reflected this history. White musicians like Buddy Holly, who invented rock and roll, often drew their inspiration from living and working with black musicians. Black performers who won admiration and acclaim in the society at large were in the vanguard of social integration. The first generally accepted images of blacks and whites mingling in a relaxed social setting were of black performers entertaining white audiences.

Insofar as it broke down racial barriers, this was all to the good. Unfortunately, it had a negative side, too. Because black musicians figured so importantly as agents of racial change and representatives of the black community, their prominence tended to confirm the false notion that the subculture from which they came was the dominant culture of the black community. It perpetuated the tra-

ditional stereotype of the uninhibited black over whom sensual passion held unchallenged sway. The great black majority, for whom
life meant work and sacrifice without much promise of material
reward or many opportunities for sensual self-indulgence, disap-
peared from public consciousness before, in fact, the society at
large really acknowledged its existence.

The God-fearing, family-valuing, hardworking black majority has
thus been the "invisible man" in the typical image of America. This
wasn't just an interesting social phenomenon. It affected social
analysis and policy. It led to a pervasive tendency among academics
and others who write about blacks to stress black deficiencies and
weaknesses, while ignoring black virtues and strengths. For example, in his recent work, *The New Politics of Poverty*, Lawrence M.
Mead contends that blacks make up a disproportionate share of
the so-called underclass because "the worldview of blacks makes
them uniquely prone to the attitudes contrary to work, and thus
vulnerable to poverty and dependency."[5] To support this assertion
he offers the following historical summary of black culture:

> Group memories of slavery and Jim Crow inculcate hopeless-
> ness more powerfully than any bias blacks are likely to meet
> at present. Other groups also experienced prejudice, albeit
> less intensely. Blacks are more distinctive in how they re-
> sponded. They did not—with the exception of a few intellec-
> tuals and Black Muslims—turn away from white society and
> rely on their own enterprise to get ahead, as Jews and Asians
> did at first. Blacks did not, for example, flee the South in
> large numbers until well into this century.[6] They remained
> dependent on the white man, both economically and psy-
> chologically.[7]

Mead acknowledges that in the past, "working hard and going to
church were much of what black culture meant," but he claims

that "today, tragically, it is more likely to mean rock music or the rapping of drug dealers on ghetto street corners."

It is certainly true that some blacks, particularly among the poor, display the negative values Mead describes. But on what grounds does he contend that these attitudes are characteristic of black America as a whole? Even if we assume that all poor black Americans share them, they would not characterize the majority since, as Mead himself observes, "less than a third of blacks are poor in any given year."[8] Only a portion of those poor blacks belong to the so-called underclass from which Mead draws his conclusions about black culture. Moreover, though Mead implies that it is a thing of the past, black Americans continue to be ardent supporters of the black church:

> Based on the indices of church membership, church attendance and charitable giving in 1987, different studies have pointed out the following: about 78 percent of the black population claimed church membership and attended once in the last six months; blacks (44 percent) tend to have slightly higher rates of weekly church attendance than white Protestants (40 percent); and they have the highest rates of being superchurched (attending church more than on Sundays) among all Americans (37 percent versus 31 percent). Furthermore, if time and money are an indication of loyalty, black churches received a far higher percentage of the charitable dollar and more volunteer time than that given to any other organization by black people. The seven major black denominations have not suffered the kind of severe decline in membership experienced by some mainstream white denominations. . . .[9]

Though he implies that the influence of degenerate black cultural values "seems to lie at the origin of the underclass," Mead's discussion of black culture doesn't measure up to the importance of his subject matter. Indeed, it shows an appalling combination of bias, ignorance, and flawed reasoning. One suspects that he did little research and gave scant thought to black-American culture and character before setting down a string of deceptive generalities.

Mead treats what he regards as negative cultural values as essentially black. He implies that blacks with more positive values are exceptional, while ignoring evidence that the majority of blacks do act on more positive values. He implies that blacks who act on more positive values do so only in order to impress whites, a result, no doubt, of the fact that they remain "dependent on the white man . . . psychologically." But our examination of the historical record has indicated that positive black cultural values exist *in spite* of everything done by white racists to discourage them, during slavery and afterward. Black-American moral values developed largely in the context of spiritual and psychological resistance to the degrading assumptions and stereotypes of white racism. The main vehicle for this resistance was the black church. Yet aside from an allusion to black church attendance, Mead entirely disregards the black church. The index to his book contains no reference to black churches or religion. Thus, he purports to discuss black culture without taking seriously the institution that has mainly embodied the values and activities of the black community throughout our history.

When Mead looks at the black community, he ignores the important role of positive black values. He sees the community's weaknesses, but treats its strengths as if they must have some external origin. He suggests that negative attitudes in the black community come from black culture and experience, while positive ones come from or are inspired by whites. He asserts this view despite the existence of abundant historical evidence to the contrary. Mead may be right to reject the deterministic approaches that make racism or the lack of sufficient economic opportunities the main explanation for the plight of the so-called underclass. He may be on the right track when he sees today's hard-core poverty rooted in problems of attitude and character. His logic fails, though, when he treats black cultural values as an independent cause, while acknowledging that the values he is discussing represent a change from the past. If the values practiced by some poor blacks now differ from values held by blacks in the past, or from those held by other blacks today, facile references to black culture can't explain the difference. In fact, in light of the history we have considered so far, we are left looking for some way to explain how so many blacks today have been cut off from the values that were traditionally important to the community, values that allowed blacks to endure even worse adversity than most are facing today.

In his book, *The Promised Land*, Nicholas Lemann offers an explanation for the negative values Mead sees as the chief cause of black urban poverty. Lemann argues that such values characterized blacks who lived under the sharecropper system in the South. He contends that when the "Great Migration" brought blacks to northern cities in the middle decades of the century, it transferred as well the aberrant social behavior of the southern black sharecropper. Lemann offers very little systematic evidence for this theory. For instance, in his discussion of the black family and black sexual mores, he cites the impressions of a few academics who visited the South in the 1930s, as well as one very limited survey of 612 black families in rural Georgia by a black sociologist, Charles S. Johnson. He also appears to rely on the prejudiced conceptions of southern whites at the time.

> The white interpretation of the sharecroppers' sex lives was that they were governed by the principle of absolute lack of inhibition: everybody was sleeping with everyone else whenever the impulse arose. Short-lived common-law couplings and illegitimate children were the inevitable (and for many planters, the desired) result. Every aspect of black social life on the plantations, as whites saw it, had a brazen sexual cast.[10]

Lemann's presentation suggests that the observations of the presumably disinterested academics confirmed these prejudices. According to their writings, the black sharecropper community was characterized by promiscuity, a weak matriarchal family structure, and high rates of illegitimacy. Their description sounds remarkably like the view of the black family during slavery that prevailed until the 1970s. Lemann says that these academics "assumed they were seeing the continuation of a pattern of family life that began during slavery." He notes in passing that "a generation of historical scholarship—most notably Herbert Gutman's *The Black Family in Slavery and Freedom*—stands in refutation of the idea that slavery destroyed the black family." He admits that "it is somewhat mysterious where the structure of the sharecropper family came from, if the observers of it described it accurately; but they do provide a few guesses besides the legacy of slavery." The guesses include "the planters' idea of the lazy, carefree sharecropper," the sharecropper system's destruction of black self-esteem, and "the relative economic independence of poor black women as a destabilizing influence on families." Lemann concludes that "whatever the cause of its differentness, black sharecropper society on the eve of the introduction of the mechanical cotton picker was the equivalent of big-city ghetto society today in many ways."[11] Finally, Lemann cites work by W.E.B. Du Bois and black scholar E. Franklin Frazier (the latter being the authority heavily relied on by the Moynihan report) to prove that "when patterns of family disorganization appeared in black neighborhoods, they were routinely explained as a matter of recent migrants from the rural South bringing their old way of life with them to the city."[12]

Given the way in which he presents his case, we are forced to suspect Lemann's intentions. He quotes racist views or preconceptions about blacks, cites questionable evidence that confirms these views, but fails to digest the more solid scholarship that contradicts them. He follows a similar pattern when discussing the supposed lack of strong family values among the premigration black poor. He cites "the catechism of the defenders of segregation" to the effect that "blacks were sexually uncontrollable." He concludes that "the poor blacks' way of life . . . caused the middle-class blacks to suffer the humiliation and economic loss that went with second-class citizenship." Again, racist views are used to establish a supposed fact. Then, without questioning these views, Lemann describes the consequences of the supposed fact. In this case, the effect is to blame blacks' second-class status during the Jim Crow era on the behavior of poor blacks, rather than the society's tolerance for attitudes and injustices perpetuated by racist whites. This gives new meaning to the phrase "blaming the victim."

Though Lemann alludes to Herbert Gutman's work, he writes as if it has no bearing on the issue of black family values during the sharecropper era. Yet at one point, Gutman deals explicitly with the very theory Lemann relies on. He cites an argument by white sociologist E. W. Burgess, which he says "summed up much of the conventional view of early-twentieth-century Afro-Americans." The Negro, said Burgess, "with 'his simple and loose familial and social organization has migrated en mass' to the northern cities." But Gutman contends that "Burgess and so many like him were wrong. The typical Afro-American household changed its shape in the half century between 1880 and 1930. But at all times—and in all settings—the typical black household (always a lower-class household) had in it two parents and was not 'unorganized and disorganized.' "[13] Gutman goes on to cite substantial evidence from various urban and rural settings to support this conclusion. Blacks got heavily involved in the sharecropper system in the decade following the Civil War. Thus, the period Gutman alludes to is the same period during which Lemann claims there was widespread degeneracy among poor southern blacks. Gutman's conclusions, based on quantitative analysis of census and other records on tens of thousands of black families, contradicts the theory Lemann adopts.

Gutman directly challenges the notion that black migration from the South transplanted a degenerate sharecropper culture to the northern cities.

> At all moments in time between 1880 and 1925—that is, from an adult generation born in slavery to an adult generation about to be devastated by the Great Depression of the 1930s and the modernization of southern agriculture afterward—the typical Afro-American family was lower-class in status and headed by two parents. That was so in the urban and rural South in 1880 and in 1900 and in New York City in 1905 and 1925. The two-parent household was not limited to better advantaged Afro-Americans (rural landowners, artisans and skilled workers, and members of the tiny black middle-class elite). It was just as common among farm laborers and service workers. It accompanied the southern blacks in the great migration to the North that has so reshaped the United States in the twentieth century.[14]

Besides its lack of empirical justification, Lemann's theory also fails to account for the negative attitudes toward work that analysts like Mead see as the main cause of poverty among the underclass. The sharecropper system obviously didn't destroy the traditional black commitment to self-improvement through hard work. Blacks worked hard as sharecroppers, even though the system deprived them of most of the fruits of their labor. When they decided to migrate north, it was usually in response to the lure of jobs in the northern cities that offered a better return for their labor. The strong commitment to self-improvement that characterized blacks in previous periods was obviously an important factor in the decision to go north.

Though he is apparently aware of the facts, Lemann sticks with his derogatory theory. It provides the conceptual background for the remainder of his book, which turns out to be an extended anecdotal slander against the moral character of black Americans. For Lemann, the saga of the great migration is a story of intermittent work, promiscuity, infidelity, and broken marriages that was the precursor of today's urban nightmare. Lemann's account leaves the impression that a welfare bureaucrat and a storefront preacher represent the only blacks who managed to put together decent lives. His journalistic style lends power to his presentation, since he writes in graphic (sometimes nearly pornographic) detail about the lives of real individuals. Yet he never adequately addresses the question that should always be in the mind of the reader: How typical of the black community are the people he portrays? Millions of blacks migrated from the South. Some became factory workers or sanitation engineers. Others worked in fish markets, restaurants, and bars. Many, especially among women, continued to do domestic work just as they had in the South, and so on. Despite the limits of opportunity at a time when openly racist attitudes still prevailed in the workplace, most did not end up as welfare bureaucrats, storefront preachers, or permanent inhabitants of the welfare plantation. The majority succeeded in making relatively decent lives for themselves, and at the very least, avoided becoming part of the so-called underclass. Yet Lemann doesn't bother to tell the story of any of these families.

Like the famous (or infamous) Moynihan report,[15] both Mead and Lemann choose to accentuate the negative. They adopt a negative portrait of black-American character and values, even though evidence they choose to ignore contradicts the negative portrayal. Also like Moynihan before them, these writers use their work to argue the need for government action to deal with the negative situation they describe. Mead sees the need for "a reassertion of public authority."

The frontier for a new liberalism, therefore, must be the welfare state, not other public institutions or the economy. It is partly in return for benefits that government might seek to enforce behaviors, such as work, that sustain trustful inter-actions among citizens.[16]

Lemann advocates what he calls "a wholesale government effort, an effort so comprehensive that it would stand a good chance of substantially affecting the life of everyone who lives in the ghettos."

Obviously the precise conception and management of all the programs require painstaking, detailed work, but the overall concept is simple and direct: the government should be trying to break the hold on individuals of those aspects of ghetto culture that work against upward mobility, by providing a con-stant, powerful force that encourages the people of the ghet-tos to consider themselves part of the social structure of the country as a whole.[17]

Mead and Lemann portray black culture and values as the prob-lem, forceful government intervention as the solution. People who advocate such a strategy often call themselves liberals, but from a black point of view, their approach is anything but progressive. Though dressed in new clothes, it represents essentially the same approach America has taken toward blacks since slavery times. Since blacks are deficient in character and cannot take care of themselves, some outside force must be invoked to provide the discipline they lack. For a long time, the slave regime provided the necessary force, then the system of Jim Crow segregation. Under the supposedly liberal policies of the sixties and again today, the controlling force becomes the social welfare bureaucracy.

Though introduced to the world in the context of the freedom movement of the sixties, welfare-state liberalism, in fact, made its beneficiaries the subjects of a bureaucratic tyranny.[18] People in public housing projects have had little or no say in the affairs of their own communities. Women on welfare have had little or no authority over the affairs of their own families. Welfare entitlement regulations have made it perversely illogical for men to assume their responsibilities as husbands and fathers. In effect, the permanent beneficiaries of the liberal welfare system are diverted from their claim to be equal, responsible citizens of a self-governing democratic state. They become instead the inhabitants of an unfree, basically totalitarian "welfare state." Authorities they do not choose and over whom they have no control determine what they are permitted to eat (e.g., what food can be purchased with food stamps); where they live (e.g., under what circumstances access to public housing or rent subsidies will be available); how their families will be organized (e.g., if assistance will continue if an able-bodied male lives in the home)—and so forth. Recent changes in welfare legislation move in the direction of dictating what work recipients must do and on what terms.

Bureaucracies are inherently antidemocratic. Bureaucrats derive their power from their position in the structure, not from their relations with the people they are supposed to serve. The people are not masters of the bureaucracy, but its clients. They receive its services, but only insofar as they conform to its authority. The bureaucracy is like a computer; it responds only to those who address it in the proper form. In this sense, a bureaucratic government program has a double meaning: The program serves its clients, but it also programs them.

Thanks to this programming effect, bureaucratic government can become the enemy of self-discipline. A self-disciplined person acts in accordance with goals and priorities that reflect their own distinctive moral identity. The client of a bureaucracy has no distinctive identity. Each one is processed, and consequently takes on the characteristics demanded by the process. This has meaning beyond being assigned a number or the other superficial marks of clientage. The welfare bureaucracy, for instance, offers help to people with certain characteristics. Those who feel in need of this help will modify their behavior in order to take on the characteristics. If help goes most easily to unmarried women with one child or more, potential clients will modify their behavior accordingly, in order to become real in terms of the bureaucratic process. Where the perceived need is extensive enough, the bureaucracy may reprogram whole communities and destroy their integrity. Like a computer virus, it turns previous patterns of action in new directions. Once behavior has been modified, the client depends upon the bureaucracy for further instructions. By accepting its discipline, the client risks becoming psychologically dependent on the bureaucracy as the primary determinant of his or her goals and priorities. One starts by looking to the bureaucracy for help. One ends up unable to act without its approval.

The American welfare-state bureaucracy has not yet come to this extreme, but it's getting there. Yesterday, a single woman who had a child could turn to the state for help. Today, having grown used to the idea of pregnancy outside of marriage, the same woman learns that, in order to receive help, she must work. Tomorrow, perhaps, she will be told where and for whom. Welfare assistance is gradually transformed into welfare slavery, all in accordance with the logic of bureaucratic government.[19]

The bureaucracy reduces each client to a uniform participant in the process, like the atoms that compose a molecule. The client may have capacities that in fact distinguish her from all the other clients in the process, but the bureaucracy cannot take account of them. Though here and there particular bureaucrats may try to recognize individual distinctions, on the whole, the process does not allow it. Each client's distinctive moral identity has to give way to the uniform identity the process demands.

In a free democratic society, such as that envisaged by America's Declaration of Independence, government derives its just authority from the consent of the governed. The people are understood to be the legitimating arbiters of government power. By contrast, in the liberal welfare state, government derives its authority from the needs of the governed. The subjects of the welfare state are understood to be those who, for whatever reason, are too powerless, weak, or helpless to provide adequately for themselves. The authority which orders their lives is not determined by their choice. In fact, their acceptance of this authority is understood to be the result of circumstances they do not choose, and over which they have no control.

The concept of the individual which underlies the welfare state differs fundamentally from that implied by the Declaration. In fact, it reestablishes the paternalistic view of human beings which the American founders rejected. Such paternalism had been used to justify political arrangements in which a privileged elite makes the decisions, while the majority of the people have no say. Instead of a voluntary social contract based on the primacy of individual rights, we have a forcible covenant based upon the manipulation of individual needs. In exchange for the satisfaction of needs they supposedly cannot satisfy for themselves, individuals are made to accept the authority of those who claim to have the strength, wealth, or expertise to take care of things for them. Just such a bargain provided the basis for the feudal subjection of defenseless peasants to their warrior overlords. Just such a bargain gave roots to the imperial bureaucratic despotism that ruled in China for centuries. Its logic survived into the twentieth century, to become the basic canon of totalitarian legitimacy.

We live today in an era when totalitarian systems in the Soviet Union, China, and elsewhere around the globe are collapsing beneath the accumulated weight of their hopelessly incompetent ideologies. But right here at home, communities are also being devastated by the consequences of failed totalitarianism—the covert totalitarianism of the liberal welfare state. Given the principles of individual rights and self-government on which American democracy is based, such covert totalitarianism would be wrong and unacceptable even if it could deliver on its promise to satisfy the needs of the helpless masses. But precisely because it contradicts those principles, the welfare state has failed in the United States just as surely as its more overtly vicious counterparts have failed in other countries.

At home and overseas, the most obvious manifestations of this failure are economic. This has led many people to talk as if the reasons for failure are also economic. Yet the poor performance of the Soviet economy, for example, was not just the result of poor management or lazy workers. It resulted from the fact that the Communists tried to organize the Soviet economy on the basis of a bad concept of the human person. Similarly, the poor results of the liberal welfare state are not solely the result of legislation poorly conceived, or programs poorly managed and organized. The welfare state is based upon the same bad concept of the human person. It is a concept that emphasizes human needs while neglecting human capacities. It stresses individual helplessness and weakness, undermining the sense of personal responsibility. It justifies ever greater concentrations of power in the hands of the state, leaving people each day more powerless to effect and improve their own condition. This bad concept leads to institutions and policies that disable individual initiative, motivation, and creativity. Faced with political and social structures that embody the assumption of individual impotence, individuals acquire the passive habits and expectations that go with it.

As advocates of government paternalism, analysts like Mead and Lemann avoid or deny the idea that the policies and programs of the liberal welfare state explain, or contributed greatly to, the development of negative values among blacks in the so-called underclass. If the government caused or helped to cause the problem, it's harder to make the case that massive government action can provide an effective solution. Of course, in the 1980s, conservative analysts argued quite effectively that government policy was largely, if not wholly, to blame for the apparent moral corruption of the so-called underclass. In his book *Losing Ground*, for instance, Charles Murray showed a statistical correlation between increasing poverty, illegitimacy, and crime among the poor, and the expansion of the benefits and administrative structures of the liberal welfare state. He maintained that welfare-state policies and programs had established a structure of rewards and punishments (incentives, disincentives) that encouraged immoral attitudes and behavior (out-of-wedlock births, nonwork, criminal enterprises) while discouraging decency (education, hard work, marriage, respect for the law). Murray saw no need to blame "the lower-class and black cultural influences that are said to foster high illegitimacy rates and welfare dependency." He asserts that such "social factors are not necessary to explain behavior."

> There is no "breakdown of the work ethic" in this account of rational choices among alternatives. There is no shiftless irresponsibility. . . . There is no need to invoke the spectres of cultural pathologies or inferior upbringing. The choices may be seen much more simply, much more naturally, as the behavior of people responding to the reality of the world around them and making the decisions—the legal, approved, and even encouraged decisions—that maximize their quality of life.[20]

Murray's theory avoids the need to denigrate the culture and character of black Americans. It may explain some part of the moral dissolution that has occurred among poor blacks during the past three decades. But if black behavior has always been the result of a rational calculus of material incentives and disincentives, how do we explain the fact that, when racism and discrimination severely limited the prospects of fair reward or gain, most blacks continued to strive nonetheless? Murray assumes that prior to the advent of the welfare state, blacks were dealing with a more positive incentive structure. In fact, whether under slavery or later during the Jim Crow era, most black Americans dealt with an incentive structure that fostered demoralization. The welfare state is just the latest version of the same old situation. During most of our history, blacks (who were mostly poor) made the choice for decency even when it was clear they would suffer for it. In Chapter Two, we saw how most blacks clung to the idea of family, despite the pain that it entailed. Most blacks continued to seek education, though they were discouraged or punished when they did so. They continued to work hard, even when unfairly denied decent wages or a fair return for their agricultural produce. They continued to seek advancement, despite white racist resentment and even violence against "uppity niggers" who seemed too proud, prosperous, or successful,[21] and so on.

Murray's attempt to explain the behavior of poor blacks strictly in terms of material causes falls short because it offers no basis for understanding the motivation of decent poor people; that is, people who retain self-respect and personal integrity, despite the realization that they will never escape from poverty. For most of our history, that's what decent black Americans had to do. Whatever their own efforts or achievements, a harsh regime of racial subjugation precluded material success for most blacks. Many blacks worked at menial tasks knowing full well that their hard work would always yield just enough to get by. If the prospect of material gain is the only rational motive for self-respect and moral discipline, their lives offered no such motive. Yet they continued to strive anyway because their spiritual resources made up for the lack of external material incentives. Their sense of spiritual worth inspired them to prepare and hold themselves and their offspring in readiness for a better world, a better day. Rather than live down to the racist standards imposed upon them, they lived up to the standards suggested by their faith. Of necessity, those standards placed more value on the moral qualities that sustain relations among people (e.g., love, loyalty, compassion) than on the physical or mental capacities that are the key to the mastery and manipulation of material things.

However, the establishment of strong moral values is a challenge for any community or society. This means that in any community, examples are to be found of the attitudes and behavior Lemann ascribes to poor black sharecroppers, or that Mead sees as characteristic of today's black culture. At any given moment, the moral condition of a society or social group represents a point of dynamic equilibrium between the forces that support moral integrity and those that undermine it. In the black-American community, moral integrity always had a host of factors ranged against it: slavery, racism, antiblack violence, economic subjection or discrimination, conscious efforts to deprive blacks of education, etc. Given the weight of these forces, it shouldn't be surprising that the black community has always had a somewhat harder time maintaining its basic moral structure and institutions. But we have seen that, contrary to the impression writers like Lemann and Mead want to create, black efforts to do so were largely successful; that is, until the era of large-scale welfare paternalism. Yet also contrary to what Charles Murray's theory would lead us to expect, this success did not result from a system of material incentives that supported moral behavior. It came about because black Americans evolved a system of values that gave greater weight to moral goods no one could take away than to material things they had little hope of attaining.

The history of black Americans is thus a history of resisting or rejecting the adverse structure of material incentives established by a society intent on breaking our spirit and destroying our self-respect. As part of this resistance, black Americans judged self-worth and achievement in terms of moral rather than materialistic standards. By doing so, we thwarted the system of racial discrimination and oppression that barred us from material success in order to devalue our lives and crush our spirit. Family, religious faith, and a deep commitment to self-improvement appear to be the three pillars of the black-American character. A strong sense of moral identity, based on these values, gave black Americans the wherewithal to resist despair and keep up the daily struggle to survive and advance ourselves, even when racial bigotry and discrimination severely limited our chances of success. It provided the reserve of moral courage and self-discipline that Martin Luther King successfully evoked to sustain his strategy of nonviolent resistance during the Civil Rights struggle.

Thanks to the "invisible man" syndrome affecting the decent black majority, however, this positive moral identity didn't figure in the ideas and blueprints of the social architects and engineers responsible for the explosive growth of the liberal welfare state. Some regarded blacks as helpless victims of racism and economic circumstances. Others implied that they were moral degenerates whose character had been destroyed by past oppression. All were compelled by the assumptions of their social-science methodology to see the black community through the distorting lens of scientific materialism. Modern social science is based on the notion that science deals with facts—material, quantifiable facts. Questions of value, moral questions are assumed to lie outside the purview of social-science methodology. So what does a social scientist do when he encounters a fact that is essentially moral in character; for instance, a religious institution? He breaks it down into nonmoral elements; i.e., those that abstract from its moral claims or influence. In this process, unfortunately, what gets lost is precisely what is most important about the institution as seen from within. The social scientist can count church membership and attendance. He can add up church assets and income. He can even discuss church people, insofar as they become actors on the secular stages of politics and society. But he can't deal seriously with the church's moral influence or integrity. Material things are merely incidental from the point of view of the church's moral mission. But in the social scientist's eyes they become its defining characteristics.

This methodological limitation meant that the social scientists did what blacks themselves had long resisted doing—they defined blacks in material terms, using the material condition of whites as the normative standard. By every material measure the black community was poorer and weaker than the norm. Therefore, being black became synonymous with weakness. Measured in these material terms, the black identity seemed simply oppressive and worthless, something to be lamented and eventually overcome. Since the values and institutions of the black community appeared to have produced such deficient material results, they were treated as if they, too, had no value except perhaps as social curiosities. Given this negative view of the black identity, the social engineers naturally saw their efforts to deal with the problems of the community as providing blacks with what they lacked. Blacks lacked economic status, so one strategy emphasized jobs. Blacks lacked adequate training, so another emphasized education. Blacks lacked decent housing, so another emphasized housing projects, and so forth. Finally, when their methodological blindness and negativity comes upon itself, they conclude that black culture undermines the work ethic. Therefore, what blacks need is "middle class" values, the ones that impel people to work hard so they can have more of the things money can buy.

These strategies have been worse then ineffective; they have been harmful. Sure, some of the jobs programs marginally increased black employment. Some of the training programs marginally improved the number of skilled black workers. But in exchange for such intermittent and questionable results, they enshrine and perpetuate a view of what it means to be black that is all about what blacks lack, and not at all about what they have achieved. Defeated by this negative self-image, millions of poor blacks have surrendered to the moral depression that has crushed their will to work and fostered the nihilistic spirit that fuels the urban nightmare.

The negative assumptions of the liberal social engineers forced discussion of issues affecting the black community into a mold that assumes the primacy of material standards and considerations. Given the character forged by the black-American experience, black Americans can only accept this assumption if they are willing to abandon everything their experience has taught them. On such terms, they can be successful only if they cease to be black. Somehow, instinctively, many black Americans understand this fact. This may be why they shy away from rhetoric about "middle-class values," and tolerate the idea that people who "succeed" in the way the larger American society now understands that term have somehow betrayed their black identity. It's not that material success is bad; it's just that you don't really appreciate what it means to be black if that's what you're all about. There has to be something more, something that necessarily escapes the quantitative social scientists and social engineers, something that transcends the "good things in life" to make life itself good, something that justifies effort even when material rewards are missing. This sense of a transcendent good was the foundation of black self-respect and motivation when racial injustice systematically denied blacks their fair material rewards. It may offer a foundation for motivating blacks who today are being consigned to the depths of the so-called underclass.

To build on that foundation, one would have to take seriously the black institutions that social scientists treat as an afterthought— the black churches. That's where good things are happening today in the black community. But liberal politics and ideology have produced a situation that limits the scope and influence of the churches. Any strategy for renewal in the black community must liberate them from these constraints, and in doing so, free the traditional heart and spirit of black America.

> *The world treat You mean, Lord,*
> *Treats me mean, too.*
> *But that's how things are down here,*
> *We don't know who You are.*

Chapter 8

RENEWING

THE

FOUNDATIONS

Any strategy for dealing with the contemporary crisis in black America should be based on a principle that respects black America's moral identity and heritage. Given what we have learned of the black-American strategy for survival during and in the aftermath of slavery, that principle may be summarized as the primacy of moral/spiritual over material values; and therefore, the primacy of organic institutions (e.g., family, church, neighborhood) over inorganic institutions (e.g., money, government, bureaucracy). If moral/spiritual values are primary, then relations with people are more important than power over things. What you are is more important than what you have. Moral intention is more important than material results. Those who succeed materially at the expense of others (for example, successful drug dealers, gangsters, vice peddlers, or unscrupulous business people and politicians) deserve condemnation. Those who strive to live decently and with respect for others deserve admiration, even if they appear to fail in material terms. Any of the poorest day laborers in our black past, who worked honestly to support a family, lived faithfully in the bosom of their church, and died broke, was worth more than all the flashy, cash-stuffed drug dealers, gang chieftains, and pimps who afflict our neighborhoods today.

Given this principle, black Americans who live as if money, sensual pleasure, and material power are the chief objectives of life have abandoned the essence of their black character. Black-American writers, musicmakers, and moviemakers who portray material success and power as the cynosure of happiness and achievement misrepresent their black heritage. Black-American social, economic, and political leaders who accept material advancement (i.e., more jobs and income) as the be-all and end-all of progress betray their black identity. They all surrender to the enslaving view that reduces a person's worth to what they can fetch in the marketplace. In their obsession with the effort to liberate our bodies from material need, they help to fasten and lock new shackles upon our minds and spirit. This doesn't mean that black Americans should abandon efforts to achieve material goals, or disown those who do so successfully. It means valuing such success less for what it does for the individual than for what it says about, and does for, the character of the community. This is the ethic black Americans followed in order to survive in the midst of government-sponsored racism and discrimination. It is the ethic we must rediscover in order to survive today.

Apart from the people and institutions that embody them, human moral precepts become mere abstractions that can be used as easily for evil as for good. Black Americans learned this firsthand during slavery, when their enslavers abused Christian precepts as part of the effort to facilitate physical domination by shaping the opinions and ideas black people had about themselves. To resist this effort, black Americans developed, albeit often in some hidden fashion, institutions of their own. In order to be their own, these institutions had to be based on something that blacks controlled. They had little or no control over their material circumstances. But, as defined by their Christian beliefs, they had control over the moral quality of their actions and reactions in those circumstances. Whatever the identity thrust on them by their oppressors, they could maintain a moral autonomy that transcended their oppressed condition. Family and church were the institutions that especially reflected this moral autonomy. They were the core elements of black-American identity. From the black viewpoint, therefore, these institutions are constitutive, not merely instrumental. Strong families are not valuable just because, for example, they improve one's economic prospects. Church membership isn't valuable just because it helps keep young people out of trouble with the law. Both are invaluable simply because apart from them, we lose control of who and what we are.

This poses a special problem when formulating policy for the black community, a problem that the liberal black establishment has consistently ignored. Black liberals have favored government-dominated approaches. Yet in America today, the prevalent interpretation of the doctrine of church-state separation forbids government support for projects and activities based on a religious viewpoint. The government can give money for a head-start class in the church basement, provided the curriculum doesn't include Bible study. The government can fund sex education classes for young teens, provided the syllabus doesn't teach Christian concepts of love and marriage. The government can fund job training programs, but not if they inculcate religious ideas of motivation, e.g., family obligation and responsibility. Thus, if they follow the liberal approach, in order to improve their material circumstances, blacks must reject the keystone of their ethnic identity.

In the era before liberal materialism dominated the leadership of the black community, a different approach was possible. We can see it in the histories of almost all the historically black colleges. All received support from sources outside the black community, including, in some cases, government funding. But they did not surrender their black heritage to secure this support. Christian worship and the inculcation of Christian moral values formed the center of the curriculum. The black concept of family prevailed, so that every member of the college community regarded the others as brothers and sisters for whom they were responsible. In addition to whatever knowledge and skills they acquired, students were supposed to complete the character formation that had begun in the families and churches of their home communities. They learned never to shrink from hard work, self-discipline, and self-sacrifice. They learned that in a world where so much was against them, black folks could not afford to live for themselves alone.

The ethos of black colleges reflected the moral culture of the black community. Ironically, this was partly due to the fact that black colleges developed in the context of racial segregation. Though it was bad in principle and unjust in its operation, legally enforced segregation did create an environment in which the distinctive identity of the black community was assumed, and therefore to a degree respected, especially by blacks themselves. Though whites enforced segregation as a badge of inferiority, among themselves blacks often refashioned this separateness into an expression of their self-respect. In this sense, segregation unintentionally gave the black community opportunities for moral and psychological self-possession even while it blocked many avenues of material ownership and advancement. It deprived black Americans of their rightful participation in the society at large, but it allowed (or more precisely, ignored) the black community's control over institutions that catered exclusively to blacks. Perhaps without consciously intending or realizing it, the black liberal establishment abandoned this inadvertent autonomy when it adopted integration as the paramount goal of the civil rights struggle.

At this point, it's important to think for a moment about the distinction between pursuing an end to segregation and pursuing integration. The one required that all legally enforced measures of separation and discrimination be eliminated. It was a question of justice and equity under law. The other often involved a whole set of assumptions about the relative value of one racial identity or another. These assumptions can go so far that they appear to validate the derogatory premises that led to segregation in the first place. For example, in the famous *Brown* v. *Board of Education* case, in which the Supreme Court ruled against racial segregation in education, the aim was to end segregation. However, the opinion incorporated the argument that without integration, there could be no equality. It seemed unthinkable that an educational institution that had little or no white participation was not inherently inferior. Pity the poor African countries, where there aren't enough whites to go around. The outcome of the Brown case was the right outcome, but the rationale for the decision unintentionally bespoke the very prejudice whose effects it sought to overturn.

Unless they consciously guard against it, therefore, the pursuit of the liberal agenda can lead black Americans to act without regard for their own institutions. We become so preoccupied with the negative conditions of that identity (racism, discrimination, poverty) that we lose sight of its positive moral content. In the effort to throw off the stigma of segregation, we give up the pursuit or maintenance of values that reflect the distinctive moral identity forged by the black-American experience. No black American with an authentic sense of that identity could be comfortable with a strategy that substitutes the power of government bureaucracy for the autonomous action and influence of the black churches. Yet this is precisely what the liberal black establishment has done. The institutions that were central to black survival and communal life have become peripheral and subordinate to the instruments of government power and the political networks that determine who controls them. Because black Americans still support their churches in large numbers, ministers remain the key figures in the black community. But too many have been co-opted by the secular political network. They act as the government's agents in the black community, rather than as authentic representatives of the community's interests and values.

Tragically, if the present condition of their families and neighborhoods is any indication, this era of government dominance has been a disaster for many black Americans. Government projects and institutions cannot adequately address the moral dimension of life. Government-run schools cannot deal with character formation. Government-administered welfare programs cannot exert moral pressure on young parents to marry and otherwise meet their family obligations. Government-financed job-training programs cannot effectively appeal to conscience or moral aspiration to supply the defect of material motives that necessarily haunts the lives of the poor.

Of course, from the viewpoint of unrestrained individual action, bureaucratic domination can seem like liberation. A young teenage girl may want to have a child in order to create a situation in which she no longer has to rely on parents or other relations for daily sustenance. This emboldens and exacerbates the ordinary rebelliousness of adolescence, feeding the conviction that she doesn't have to alter her behavior in order to placate their sensibilities, and helping to destroy whatever authority responsible older relatives might have over her. It may also reduce or eliminate altogether any sense of responsibility toward her on the part of the male partner in conception. Since bureaucratic relief is handy, he doesn't have to be. Neither the young woman nor her partner feel they have to mollify the moral sentiments of the decent majority. They feel no shame. The bureaucratic relief system doesn't require it. The needs and feelings occasioned by their conduct no longer draw them back toward a community where feelings of family obligation, or the pressures of religious feeling provide an incentive to work, set a responsible example, or provide for the future.

The bureaucratic definition of the family has no moral content. The biological tie which is only the starting point for personality in the organic family, becomes the only point of personality in the bureaucratic definition. Being a parent no longer means being a responsible, responsive influence. Even where the bureaucracy tries to take account of this part of its meaning, the effort proves administratively impossible. Moral phenomena cannot easily be expressed in terms that fit on bureaucratic forms. The bureaucracy knows no happy medium, for instance, between periodically neglecting an irresponsible parent and taking her child away. It cannot establish those guardians in the mind and heart through which organic families and community-based religions of conscience monitor and guide behavior. The bureaucracy can dominate, it can intimidate, but it cannot educate or persuade.

Because of these deficiencies, bureaucratized, government-run programs and institutions cannot deal effectively with social tasks that require forming or influencing character. Government-run schools are plagued by violence and a lack of discipline; government welfare programs encourage family disintegration; government-run jobs programs do nothing to counteract the culture of hopeless idleness that flourishes in the bars and on the streets. The traditional culture and values of the black community developed precisely in order to avert these consequences of poverty and repression, but the liberal reliance on government-dominated approaches has deprived many black Americans today of access to that heritage. So by the thousands they are perishing, just as their ancestors would have perished had they surrendered to the assumptions of the system devised to subjugate them. They are dying physically from violence, drugs, and the effects of poverty, because they have never lived as moral beings, conscious of the fact that they are part of a people whose whole experience confirms their capacity to defy and overcome material subjection.

Black America will not escape the current spiral of decline and self-destruction unless we rediscover and renew our moral heritage as a people. Rising interest in the idea of Afro-centric education bespeaks the community's growing recognition of this fact. But this interest often takes forms that appear based on the belief that the rediscovery of our heritage is just a matter of intellectual or artistic consciousness and self-perception. Through merely intellectual consciousness and representation we cannot reclaim our moral selves, or reassert the moral autonomy that was the key to our ability to resist the intended degradation of slavery and racist repression. Action is the essence of moral life. To preserve our moral heritage, it is not enough to recall the facts of our past experience. We must also remember in our present actions the values they represent. At the communal level, this means reclaiming and strengthening the focal institutions through which we have lived and acted as a people.

At the heart of this process of communal renewal must be a determination to reassert black America's deeply rooted moral commitment to the marriage-based family. We should reject the sham sophistication of intellectuals who argue that the collapse of the traditional black family structure is just a new way of adapting to changing circumstances. We should also reject those who blithely declare that these changes are just part of a transformation taking place in the society as a whole. The family system offers the primary alternative to dependency upon the power of others, and the most reliable refuge against its abuse. Whatever form the systematic subjugation of black Americans has taken, it has always included an attack on the family structure. How can anyone believe that the present disintegration of the black family does not work toward the same destructive purpose?

The marriage-based family is a natural, almost organic social whole. It springs from, and is originally bound together by, instinctive urges. But human beings react self-consciously to instinct. The bonds we form because of it transform us, by transforming the ideas we have about ourselves. Through the family we have our primordial experiences of ecstasy and power, of helplessness and obligation. Through the family we remold the world, and are remolded by it, but always in our own image, the image of human life unfolding. Parents see themselves renewed in their children. Children discover themselves in their relationship with their parents. In the context of family life, each individual struggles to unite the disparate yet similar aspects of their humanity—male and female, mother and father, daughter and son—the self we were and are, the self we will, and yet can never, be. We see something of ourselves on either side of this opposition, so the conflict inherent in family life may be painful, but it is never without significance for our moral identity.

People who develop their individuality in the context of the marriage-based family develop at the same time into complex social beings. The individual personality represents an internalized social whole, in which the influences of different family members are woven into the fabric of need, passion, and unconscious thought. The equilibrium among these influences determines the stability of the personality. The inevitable tension generated by their combination and interaction determines its energy and motivational resources. The hierarchy among them affects its strength and concentration.

Whatever the material conditions and circumstances in which the family exists, strong characters can emerge from a strong family environment. This is one reason why poverty does not, by itself, explain the crime, violence, and drug abuse that plagues many urban neighborhoods. Among African Americans, for instance, prolonged and prevalent poverty did not produce these effects as long as the family system maintained its integrity. This coincided with the period during which segregation and discrimination forced the community to rely upon its own institutional resources. Through the system of church-based self-government, the decent portion of the community exerted leadership and influence. The churches' moral influence reinforced the family system. In turn the churches acquired strength from the membership, activity, and material support of the families that built their social lives around them. This is not to say that the African-American community, or any other for that matter, was composed entirely of decent, family-oriented, churchgoing people. But family-oriented, church-based self-government meant that individuals who wanted to call upon the resources of the community for help had to deal with such people.

Theirs were the governing mores, and they generated a moral force strong enough to keep poverty or injustice from producing general moral dissolution.

The end of segregation, the emergence of a mass-consumption economy, and the dominance of a bureaucratic welfare state tended to weaken or subvert the position and practical moral authority of the black community's church-based, family-oriented institutions. The liberal black establishment's preoccupation with national politics and national solutions greatly reenforced this tendency. At the national level, where American homogeneity and unity command at least symbolic allegiance, every group has to surrender or camouflage the distinctive values and institutions that are the basis of ethnic identity. This is the practical meaning of the doctrine of church-state separation. The Irish Kennedys veiled their Catholicism; the southern Carters, their Baptist fundamentalism. By making national politics its primary focus, liberal leadership forces the black community to take a position that makes it seem as if this compromised identity is all that exists. Yet in fact, the black community is Christian in much the same sense that the Jewish community is Jewish. Our religion is at the core of our being as a people. Individual blacks who seek the meaning of their ethnicity must come to terms with it one way or another, even if they ultimately decide to neglect or reject it. This holds true at the communal level as well. To find the black community, you must go first into the churches. But if we accept the assumption of the liberal establishment that for blacks, all politics is national politics, and if, at the national level, the doctrine of church-state separation banishes the activity and authority of religious institutions as such, doesn't liberalism necessarily involve the abandonment of our most essential characteristic?

After thirty years of liberal misrule, the black community today is overgrown by a complex web of external entanglements and dependencies. The area of autonomy virtually forced upon us by legal segregation is a thing of the past. From welfare to student aid, from minority set-asides to housing subsidies, black Americans are offered a tempting array of supposed benefits. To secure these benefits, however, they must deal with an often complex and unyielding bureaucratic maze, which absorbs and defeats their best efforts. Of course, at the moment of greatest frustration, the political system kicks in, offering ways to negotiate the maze, in exchange for personal or institutional subordination. The control once achieved by external means, through segregation and the force of law, is now achieved by apparently more positive inducements. But the new subjection is even more complete, because it rests on an appearance of racial progress that makes it possible to deny the need for any sphere of black autonomy. People who insist on that need are stigmatized as separatists, crypto-segregationists who foment discord and division by rejecting the ideal of racial integration.

As long as people see the black identity as a purely negative consequence of external oppression, this criticism of the pursuit of black autonomy may be justified. As a negative fact, black ethnicity is defined in opposition to the oppressor, the racial enemy. Louis Farrakhan, or militant rappers like Sister Souljah and Public Enemy represent this kind of thinking. They appear to accept the ultimately self-degrading view that the only thing black Americans have in common is their heritage of oppression. This naturally leads to the belief that the only reliable passion we share in common is hatred of the oppressor. Hatred sustains two possible responses: avoidance or destruction of the hated object. So this negative view of the black ethnicity culminates in strategies that envisage violent conflict and, eventually, physical separation from "white dominated" American society. Of course, from a black viewpoint, both these outcomes are self-destructive delusions. If we define the enemy as nonblack American society, it is clearly an enemy blacks aren't strong enough to defeat by violence. So the impulse stirred by the rhetoric of hate feeds black-on-black violence instead. Physical separation, even if it were possible, would most likely mean confinement to a racial ghetto with all the disadvantages of today's predominantly black urban centers, but no avenues of distraction or hope of eventual escape.

For all their seeming militancy, therefore, those who base their actions on the negative view of black ethnicity aren't true militants at all. The most militant approach is the one that works, not one that leads to self-defeat and self-destruction. But the negative view of black ethnicity is not the only alternative. In the course of this work, we have come to see the black moral identity as a positive reality, based on values that sustain both individual achievement and community cooperation. The idea of black autonomy need not, therefore, entail violence, or an effort to separate ourselves from "the enemy." It can mean, instead, an effort to develop communities that reflect and preserve the moral character that emerged from black-American experience. In pursuing this goal, black Americans can act out of respect for ourselves, not hatred of others.

The new concept of black autonomy also requires that we free ourselves from the assumption that black problems require national solutions. This assumption made sense when the early Civil Rights movement leaders called on the power of the federal government in the efforts to overthrow legal discrimination and segregation. It makes no sense when dealing with the problems that beset neighborhoods and communities today. Neighborhood problems need neighborhood solutions—approaches devised and carried into action by the people affected. Of course, that's easy to say, but it hardly seems feasible when the people living in the neighborhoods lack the power to do anything about their situation. Therefore, the new concept of black autonomy leads back to the concern with power, and the distribution of power, that characterized some black thinking in the late sixties. Power is the necessary but not sufficient basis of all responsibility. People without power cannot take responsibility for themselves or their community.[1]

But the concept of power has to be understood in light of the principle of our black identity, the principle that gives primacy to the organic institutions that best reflect our moral selves. The challenge implied by the new concept of black autonomy is therefore to restore to decent people in our urban neighborhoods the power they need to establish and maintain their moral integrity and authority. Neither warmed-over socialism nor primarily economic strategies of empowerment address this challenge, since they rest on an essentially materialistic concept of power. Though some liberals see the need for community action, their obsession with national solutions keeps them from promoting the development of power at the appropriate, grassroots level. Some conservatives see the need for empowerment, but their preoccupation with individual economic solutions keeps them from promoting the development of community-based institutions. One side sees government action as the main solution; the other sees it mainly as part of the problem. Neither has rediscovered the concept that alone provides for the restoration of the community's moral power through an effective combination of private enterprise and community self-government at the grassroots level.

This concept is a rediscovery in two senses. It was the basis for much of the thinking that originally shaped the Great Society concept of community action. It was also the basis for much of America's success in maintaining a democratically governed republic during the nineteenth century. Alexis de Tocqueville writes insightfully about the critical importance of local self-government as the foundation of American democracy. Local government is the classroom and laboratory of democratic freedom. Only by participating in the decisions that shape the local community in which they live do people experience firsthand the meaning of democratic power and the sense of responsibility it should entail. The feelings of security, trust, and fulfillment they develop concretely at the local level become the foundation for their allegiance and patriotism toward the national community, which necessarily remains something of an abstraction. As a matter of tangible, daily reality, people don't live in a nation. They live in a neighborhood. How they feel about the nation depends to a large degree on how they feel about their neighborhood. If they play no role at all in governing their neighborhood, democracy is a cruel deception.

In the local governments that Tocqueville describes, people elected representatives to make local laws, enforce them, and pass judgment upon those who violated them. Thanks to the leadership and coordination of these representatives, the inhabitants of the neighborhood could join together in support of projects necessary for the community's welfare, such as building schools, developing and maintaining roads, and the like. The inhabitants of the neighborhood could feel that they had an opportunity to influence what happened in their community, because they had direct access to their representatives, and could work to remove them if they failed to perform satisfactorily. Thanks to this direct access, they could also call upon the cooperation and common resources of the community in support of projects they felt would serve the public good. Individuals were moved to take the initiative precisely because they knew where to turn to get others to join them. The institutions of local self-government provided a meeting ground for the community's leaders. People active in churches or service organizations could join forces with decent business and working people, civic-minded professionals, and interested home and property owners.

This meant that decent people in the community did not feel isolated in their struggle to establish and maintain the moral and material integrity of their lives. This extended even to physical defense against criminal elements, since each citizen might be armed and could participate in the militia (or later, the *posse comitatus*), which was the neighborhood's citizen police force. Through the jury system, every citizen also had the right to participate in the administration of justice Each could aspire as well to be a neighborhood magistrate, or justice of the peace. In a concrete sense, each and every citizen could claim a share in the community and its institutions, through which they were incorporated to form an organic political whole.

Thanks to its reliance on bureaucratic government, the liberal welfare state inhibits or precludes the development of this kind of community self-government. But bureaucratic domination could not keep people from reaching for it, even in the poorest communities. In the 1980s, a few such individuals spearheaded the tenant management movement in some public housing projects. For the first time since the early days of the Great Society program, a government-backed effort resulted in the establishment of grassroots institutions of self-government at the neighborhood level. The positive results have been striking and are by now quite well known. Yet even the Republicans who championed tenant management seem to have missed its real significance. Community empowerment, through institutions of self-government, creates the conditions for individual empowerment through economic opportunity. By giving decent people in the community a corporate, institutional identity (in this case, in the form of tenant management councils), tenant management restored their ability to define a communal identity that could resist the forces of moral dissolution.

The tenant management model is, however, only a hint in the right direction. The fully developed project of neighborhood self-government takes the model out of the public housing projects into neighborhoods where bureaucratic reprogramming is less explicit. It begins with a definition of the neighborhood, and includes a description of the institutions through which to empower its decent inhabitants.

A *neighborhood* is an area defined so that a representative body chosen by the people of the area includes only individuals who live in and with the same conditions as the people who selected them. Geographically, the area may be large or small, densely or sparsely populated, depending on the homogeneity of the living conditions of the people in question. In practice, though, the people who live in the neighborhood have the best understanding of its defining boundaries.

Each neighborhood should elect a neighborhood council, or governing body, which would be empowered to pass ordinances concerning the peace, order, and welfare of the neighborhood. This body would have the power to levy a small tax on the gross revenues of persons doing business from premises located in the neighborhood, and to appoint such administrative and clerical staff as deemed necessary to carry on the neighborhood's affairs.

Each neighborhood should elect a sheriff or neighborhood constable charged with recruiting and organizing a neighbor watch or constabulary. The sheriff and those he appoints should receive a course of training, at the police academy of the city, county, or state in which the neighborhood is located. His salary, and that of his deputies, should be paid out of funds raised by or allocated to the neighborhood council, to whom he should answer for all raises, citations, or other forms of reward or recognition. The council would also hear and adjudicate any complaints brought against him or his deputies by residents of the neighborhood. In addition to his deputies, the sheriff would be responsible for identifying, training, and organizing an auxiliary force of neighborhood residents to act as a militia, or *posse comitatus*, that would aid the constable and his deputies as they deem appropriate in the performance of their neighborhood watch. The neighborhood constabulary would rely upon the professional police force of the city, county, or state in which the neighborhood is located for aid, and would be subject to the jurisdiction of these police forces when dealing with matters that pertain to violations of city, county, or state law, the apprehension of fugitives from other jurisdictions, etc.

Each neighborhood should elect one or more justices of the peace or local magistrates to consider and adjudicate violations of neighborhood ordinances. These magistrates should be empowered to impose sentences including fines, confiscations, periods of neighborhood service, etc.

In addition to these basic institutions, federal and state governments should work cooperatively with neighborhood councils expeditiously to transfer the administration of social welfare programs for neighborhood residents into the hands of persons chosen by and answering to the neighborhood councils. The councils would receive federal or state funds to administer the programs, and would be subject to guidelines and oversight from federal or state governments. However, they should be given reasonable autonomy and flexibility in applying these guidelines to suit neighborhood conditions and circumstances.

In addition to handling relations with other neighborhood governments and other levels of government, neighborhood councils should be empowered to maintain relations with the business sector. To support this role, the councils should be given initial jurisdiction over the application of certain zoning and other ordinances within the neighborhood, subject to review by appropriate city, county, or state bodies.

From this bare sketch of its basic institutions and functions we cannot begin to understand the importance of neighborhood self-government. That requires a more detailed consideration of its impact upon the various elements of the community's life. Its most dramatic effect should, of course, be on the actual and potential leadership elements of the community. At last they will have a visible, community-based platform of authority from which to exert their influence. As things stand today, even where such leadership elements are active, their work is almost invisible and largely bereft of formal legitimacy. Their presumed right to speak for the community results from the sufferance of the outside institutions they deal with, not the suffrage of those they represent. This makes them suspect, even though they belong to the community, and often have its vital interests at heart. Lacking formal legitimacy, they must frequently reestablish their authority in other ways. In order to prove that they have not been coopted by outside forces, they may take strident public stands against them. At the same time, in order to get support for community projects, they must approach these same outsiders as supplicants.

Neighborhood self-government would help to resolve this dilemma. As elected representatives of the neighborhood, leaders would not be under constant pressure to prove their legitimacy. Working from a base that includes independent resources, they would be able to undertake at least some community actions without begging outsiders for support. They would also derive authority from their oversight role in the administration of law enforcement and government social welfare programs in the neighborhood. The neighborhood council would make visible the efforts and will of the community's decent inhabitants. It would provide them with an institutional focus and rallying point. Because it would exercise real legislative and administrative functions, it would have greater credibility, and attract greater participation than the merely advisory bodies that exist, for instance, in the District of Columbia.

Through the authority of the neighborhood council, the community could assert its ownership of institutions and agencies that are today regarded as representatives of outside domination. This should be especially true of the police. Existing police represent the community's estrangement from power and control. The neighborhood constables would represent the community's authority over itself. Knowing that they can better control the constables, decent residents would greet them with trust and support rather than fear. Increased support should also result from the fact that the constables reside in the community and share its life.

Unlike existing police forces, neighborhood constables would see themselves as agents of the neighborhood community. They should be drawn from the portion of the community that has already proven individually resistant to moral dissolution. They should themselves have families, homes, or other tangible ties in the community. Though this might make them more vulnerable to intimidation, it would also increase their stake in defeating the criminal menace. Given what is happening on the streets right now, there is no reason to assume that physical courage will be in short supply. Young men and women court death today over nothing. What right have we to assume that tomorrow, none will be found to face risks for the sake of reclaiming control over their streets and homes?

Indeed, the idea of a neighborhood constabulary might be one way to harness the qualities of leadership, courage, and loyalty that are now misspent in gang competition and warfare.

As it stands, the only visible authorities the young see on the streets are the criminals or the police. The decent folk caught in the crossfire appear helpless and contemptible. In general, the institution of neighborhood self-government should provide an opportunity for decent older people in the neighborhoods to appeal for the allegiance and respect of younger residents. It should provide a venue for cooperation across generational lines, with some semblance of pride restored to the older generation. By restoring a judicial authority to the neighborhood level, neighborhood self-government arms this pride with something more than appearances.

The institution of neighborhood magistrates should especially benefit younger offenders. The existing judicial and penal systems have, in effect, become training camps for the criminal empire. The ability to survive this training, and to master the alien world in which it takes place, becomes a source of perverse pride and a sense of superiority. Today, the judicial process appears to confirm the belief that criminal acts are blows struck against domination by outsiders. Being subject to a neighborhood magistrate, younger offenders would be reminded that their actions injure their own community. The local magistrate could also impose punishments that redirect their attention and energies back toward the community.

The establishment or restoration of neighborhood authority could also pave the way for reform of the parole system. Instead of paroling prisoners into the care of a cynical yet inattentive bureaucracy, society could require that any parole be contingent on the willingness of the offender's neighborhood council to accept custody of the parolee. Grants of parole would therefore reflect a judgment by people in a specific community that the early release was acceptable to them. Neighborhood councils should also be given authority to revoke such paroles if and when they decide the offender has again become a threat to decency and order in the neighborhood. Once the community takes responsibility for the parolee, the neighborhood council and constabulary, and indeed all interested citizens in the neighborhood would, in effect, act as parole officers. This arrangement would also give the criminal elements something to fear, or gain, from their fellow citizens.

Both the unrest in Los Angeles in 1992, and the episode of injustice that occasioned it, focus our attention on the black community's vulnerability to violence, as well as its lack of trust in, and control over, law enforcement and the judiciary. But its most important weakness may be the fact the community itself has no authority over the many government programs that affect individuals in the neighborhood. Because of this deficiency, there is no connection between the help the individual receives and the decent mores the community needs to encourage. Neighborhood self-government makes it possible to rectify this deficiency by placing the administration of these programs under the jurisdiction of the representative neighborhood body, and in the hands of people from the neighborhood itself. This is especially important given the trend toward tougher conditionality in the administration of welfare programs. States are imposing work requirements, placing limits on the duration of welfare benefits, the number of children eligible for additional benefits, etc. One reform proposal would require that an unwed mother identify the father of her child before she can receive benefits. These steps represent a long-overdue effort to stem the welfare's system's erosion of individual responsibility. On the negative side, however, bureaucratic administration of a system that includes such conditions will create for the poor an environment indistinguishable from totalitarian tyranny, a Kafkaesque nightmare of pervasive government intrusion and control.

Neighborhood-based administration of such a system will avoid this ominous consequence. Even a severe regime loses the hard edge of tyranny when people feel they have a hand in shaping it. Instead of subjection to an impersonal, unsympathetic bureaucracy that they cannot influence or control, welfare recipients would deal with people who live where they live and who answer to representatives they have a hand in choosing. Such people are more likely to know when special circumstances exist that mitigate the system's requirements. They are also more likely to know when people are shamming in order to beat the system. They will be more understanding, but also harder to deceive. As in any administrative situation, abuses are likely to occur. But instead of having to negotiate a bureaucratic maze in search of redress, welfare recipients would be able to go to their neighborhood council to seek redress before their neighbors.

In addition to the dealing with crime and the administration of government-assistance programs like welfare, a third critical element of neighborhood self-government is the community's influence over the education of the young. Nowhere are the deficiencies of the government-based, bureaucratic approach more glaringly evident. Since the 1960s, the educational results being produced by government-run schools have declined dramatically. This has been accompanied by a steady deterioration in the educational environment in government-run schools. Especially (though not exclusively) in poor urban areas, they are increasingly plagued by violence, and a lack of discipline. As usual, the supposedly expert social scientists are inventing all kinds of explanations for these trends, except the one obvious to common sense. Some say the problem is inadequate funding or low teacher salaries; others blame the students' deprived economic backgrounds or the influence of television. Yet for each such explanation, clear exceptions can be cited where good results have been produced when the same factors are present and operating.

Given what we have learned of the historic black commitment to education, black Americans should be especially suspicious of these too-facile empirical analyses. Despite poverty, woefully inadequate funds, and an environment decidedly hostile to black education, we know that black Americans consistently made progress against illiteracy in the generations following emancipation. In and of themselves, these material obstacles are no bar to educational achievement. Character formation and moral discipline were the keys that sustained black commitment to self-improvement.

In the government-run schools that predominate today, these critical elements are quite purposefully excluded. Here, again, it is the influence of the doctrine of church-state separation that has given rise to the concept of "value-free" education. It is an idea modeled after the empirical social sciences in which knowledge is supposedly developed and transmitted without reference to any religious or other moral code. Even such subjects as sex education, which many people believe intrinsically and necessarily involve moral judgments, are purportedly taught by some method that eliminates their moral dimension. In a sense, it appears that this is exactly what happens. Young people acquire information without character formation. They are encouraged to be prematurely preoccupied with their passions and desires, but without any sense of the moral faculty that can discipline and guide the passions. They learn self-awareness, but without self-control.

Black Americans should be especially wary of this approach to education. In its moral effects, it greatly resembles the approach some enslavers took toward their black captives. Sexual incontinence and other forms of undisciplined passion among the enslaved they treated indulgently, to buttress the assumption that the enslaved were permanently childlike creatures unable fully to develop their moral faculty. The absence of a capacity for self-discipline (and, therefore, the inability to act with intelligent foresight) has been used at least since Aristotle's time to prove that some people are naturally suited to be slaves. "Value-free" education may be just another name for an education approach that makes people unfit for freedom.

As we have seen already, the great black educators took a decidedly different approach, since they were determined to combat the forces keeping black Americans in subjection. Character building was the core of the black educational tradition. Here again, the reliance on government-based approaches leads to the abandonment of methods that reflect black America's distinctive moral identity. In the black community, for instance, no important enterprise is begun without prayer. Yet in the government-run schools, this cultural expression was banned by the contemporary doctrine of church-state separation. This was not always the case. At the normal school that eventually became Alabama A&M, for instance, each day began with a prayer service, even though at the time, the school received state funds just as it does today.

This reminds us that the concept of public education has undergone a radical reinterpretation in the course of this century. At one time, public support for education meant the provision of public funds for educational purposes. The money did not have to be spent in government-run schools. Federal funds disbursed for black education through the Freedman's Bureau after the Civil War, for example, went to schools run by religious groups, including the American Missionary Society and some black Christian denominations. In the past half-century, however, the educational establishment spawned by government-run schools has appropriated the term *public education* to apply only to schools under its administration. Now that notion is being challenged, as proponents of voucher systems and other forms of publicly financed subsidies for parental choice in education push their agenda.

The movement toward a broader definition of public education could offer black Americans a shot at regaining true community control of the schools in which black children are educated, and an opportunity to reassert black cultural values in education. The key to this opportunity is to allow parents, rather than bureaucracies, to decide where public educational dollars are spent. Instead of being tied to a government-run system that has long since proven its inability to meet the needs of black children, in particular, black Americans could begin to do what they did in the past: establish and run schools that embody their values and identity. This could mean, among other things, schools sponsored by black churches and denominations in which the centrality of moral guidance and character formation would be reasserted. The perception that even the poorest black parents have the wherewithal to withdraw from the government-run system may also spur improvements in that system's responsiveness and results. Overall, it would allow black parents to work toward an educational process in which it is once again clear that schools belong to the community, not to government-based education bureaucrats.[2]

NOTES

CHAPTER 1: THIS LITTLE LIGHT OF MINE

1. Scanzoni, p. 5.
2. Billingsley, *Black Families*, p. 49.
3. Frazier, p. 15. For further citations along these lines, see Herskovits, pp. 3–6.
4. See Blassingame; Billingsley, *Black Families*; Fogel and Engerman; Genovese.
5. Genovese, p. xvi.
6. Mellon, p. 42.
7. Moses Grandy, *Narrative of the Life of Moses Grandy*, as quoted in Frazier, p. 36.
8. "In a world in which black women regularly had to strip to the waist to be whipped and sometimes had to strip naked to be displayed at auction, it was no small matter that they could mingle shame with their bitter resentment." Genovese, p. 471.
9. Herskovits argues against the view that the black American population came from all over Africa. He cites evidence to suggest that it was drawn primarily from the West African coast, an area with notable linguistic and cultural commonalities (see especially pp. 35–36).

10.   This is not to say that the African heritage of black Americans is not an important ingredient in this identity. As we shall see, scholars now agree that African survivals significantly influenced black American culture.

11.   The reader should note that throughout the text, a conscious effort has been made to avoid use of the term *master*, which in itself implies acceptance of the enslaver's viewpoint. Similarly, I have used the term *enslaver* rather than *slaveholder*, since the former better reflects the active role and moral responsibility of those who kept black people in captivity.

12.   Though black children often played in "promiscuous equality" with white children, they awoke to the painful realities of slavery as they began to assume slave tasks. One former slave, Lunsford Lane, described it well: "When I began to work I discovered the difference between myself and my master's white children. They began to order me about, and were told to do so by my master and mistress. . . . Indeed all things now made me feel, what I had before known only in words, that *I was a slave*. Deep was this feeling, and it preyed upon my heart like a never dying worm. I saw no prospect that my condition would ever be changed." Blassingame, pp. 185–186.

13.   Billingsley, *Black Families*, p. 69: "The destitution and disease among the Negroes, who were now uncared for and had no facilities to care for themselves, was so great that the editor of a famous newspaper observed with considerable glee that 'The Child is already born who will behold the last Negro in the State of Mississippi.' And Mississippi had more Negro slaves than any other state. The eminent southern scholar Dr. K. C. Marshall expressed a similar and more general hypothesis: 'In all probability New Year's day on the morning of the 1st of January, 1920, the colored population in the South will scarcely be counted.' "

14.   Billingsley, *Jacob's Ladder*, p. 21: "A majority of black working class and middle class individuals live in the inner cities of the nation and not in the white suburbs."

15.   Ibid., p. 66: "Internal strife has made homicide the leading cause of death for young black men, just ahead of preventable accidents and just behind suicide. Domestic strife causes unprecedented numbers of African-American mothers and fathers to war against their own children, against each other, and against their parents. Child abuse, sibling abuse, spouse abuse, elder abuse and fratricide—while by no means unique to black people—are relatively new in such numbers."

16. Ibid., p. 162: "Most cases of homicide occur inside the black community where both victim and perpetrator are black. This is true of 95 percent of black homicides. A generation ago, blacks who were murdered were more likely to be murdered by the white authorities or vigilantes."

17. Ultimately, this surrender takes its most extreme form in the vociferous support of some blacks for so-called abortion rights. Since many black children will be born poor, the argument goes, it's especially important that abortion be available to poor black mothers. The implication is that the life of a poor black child is worthless, but would not be worthless if born into better circumstances. This turns the logic of economic determinism from a justification for slavery into an argument for self-inflicted genocide.

18. Wilson, pp. 151–52.

19. Ibid., p. 156. An interesting, and in this context not wholly irrelevant, question comes to mind about how this concept of class applied to blacks during slavery when, for the most part, they were supposed to participate in the market rather in the same way the turkey participates in our Thanksgiving dinners. What does it mean to speak of class when you *yourself* (not your talent, product, or labor) are the commodity?

20. Such a conclusion is refuted by numerous real-life examples. One is this account of the family background of Carl B. Stokes, who became mayor of Cleveland: "Stokes was born in the slums of Cleveland. His father, a laundry worker, died when he was one year old. His mother alternated between working as a maid and receiving public welfare assistance, making Stokes the only mayor of a large city who was supported as a child by AFDC. While his mother worked, he and his brother were cared for by their grandmother. Both he and his brother became distinguished attorneys. The strong commitment his mother had to education, plus the opportunities provided by World War II and big city politics are among the screens of opportunity which enabled these very able young men to move from the lower class into the upper class within the span of a few years. Stokes has told how he had to hide books under his clothes as he brought them from the library, because in his neighborhood reading books was 'against the mores.' " Billingsley, *Black Families*, p. 128.

21. Of course, many social scientists will now agree that moral factors are important, and then go on to argue that positive norms go along with higher income status. This has become such a pervasive assumption that some even refer to the norms as "middle-class values." Throughout our

history, most blacks have been working-class people, yet they also learned and practiced these so called "middle-class values." Moral decency wasn't and needn't be a function of *economic* class status. In fact, it might be useful to develop a different understanding of class, one based on normative rather than economic characteristic. Such an idea of class would make better sense of the situation, for example, of the poor nobility in England. It would allow for the existence of a "natural aristocracy" whose members might exist at any income level and emerge from any social class.

CHAPTER 2: ALL IN THE FAMILY

1. Livy, p. 119.

2. Mucius claimed that three hundred others, of like mind, were involved in a conspiracy to assassinate the king, but from Livy's account, it seems that he acted alone. One of today's empirical sociologists, applying contemporary methods, might do a survey of attitudes among Roman males, between ages fifteen and twenty-five, with questions aimed at determining their attitudes toward patriotically self-inflicted pain. She would, of course, keep careful records of family income, occupation, and other indicators of economic class in order to observe significant correlations. With a good computer and a little time, she would probably be able to establish that Mucius's act was an isolated instance traceable to the aberrant social psychology of the Roman upper-middle class. Not exactly the stuff of legend. But then, what sociologist could have seen in the backward village of Rome, or later in the bare, rustic tents of the Mongols, the spirit and character to produce two of the largest land empires the world has ever known?

3. Referring to the science of his day, social reformer Marcus Garvey summed it up well: "The custom of these anthropologists is whenever a black man, whether he be Moroccan, Algerian, Senegalese or what not, accomplishes anything of importance, he is no longer a Negro. The question therefore suggests itself, 'Who and what is a Negro?' The answer is, 'A Negro is a person of dark complexion or race, who has not accomplished anything and to whom others are not obligated for any useful service.'" Brotz, pp. 560–61.

4. Frazier, p. 39.

5. Moynihan, *The Negro Family*.

6. In addition to empirical data, the Moynihan report quoted the work

of famed black sociologist E. Franklin Frazier, with whose name it has therefore been associated ever since. But Anthony Platt argues convincingly that Moynihan selectively abused Frazier's writings, and that in fact, Frazier had a more complex and nuanced view of the Negro family than the one presented in the report. Platt acknowledges, however, that Frazier "focused extensively on the disorganized Afro-American family in all its historical forms . . ." and that "there are some serious problems with Frazier's use of disorganization as an analytical construct": Platt, p. 138. Perhaps these problems made his work a ripe candidate for exploitation when Moynihan prudently went looking for a black authority to back up his analysis.

7.   Moynihan was reportedly influenced by the work of historian Stanley Elkins, who published a history of slavery in 1959. See Lemann, pp. 172–73. Elkins intended his work as an attack on slavery, but to accomplish this, he relied heavily on the view that enslaved blacks were simply devastated and dehumanized by it. His work is a prime example of an attack on a racist institution that inadvertently accepts and perpetuates its racist assumptions.

8.   In his account of the controversy the report generated, Lemann suggests that in liberal political circles people didn't try to refute the report, they simply dismissed it, along with the important subjects it raised. Lemann concludes: "The practical effect of the controversy over it was exactly the opposite of what Moynihan intended—all public discussions in mainstream liberal circles of issues like the state of the black family and the culture of poverty simply ceased." Lemann, p. 177.

9 .   Lemann, p. 177.

10.   Billingsley, *Jacob's Ladder*, p. 130.

11.   Lemann, pp. 176–77.

12.   This is especially true of the claim, traceable to the work of E. Franklin Frazier, that slavery resulted in a predominantly matriarchal family pattern among blacks. "Gutman and others have conducted a variety of sophisticated studies to demonstrate that Frazier overcounted the female-headed households among slave and antebellum black families. On this point there is little dispute." Platt, p. 142.

13.   Billingsley, *Jacob's Ladder*, p. 36; Murray, p. 132: "In 1959, low-income blacks lived in families very much like those of low-income whites and, for that matter, like those of middle- and upper-income persons of all races. Barely one in ten of the low-income black families was living in

a single-female family. By 1980, the 10-percent figure had become 44 percent."

14. Billingsgley, *Jacob's Ladder*, p. 44.

15. Ibid., p. 137.

16. Billingsley, *Black Families*, p. 85.

17. The first dramatic decline takes place between 1975 and 1981. Thus, it is possible to argue that the Carter era economic malaise was the culprit, not some general change in economic structure due to technology, etc. In all fairness, though, significant changes *were* taking place in the domestic and international economic system. True to his job title, Carter presided over America's painful reaction to those changes. One has to suspect, though, that scholars like Billingsley allow liberal ideological blinders to influence their presentation of the facts. We should also note here that the rise in the black working class preceded the dramatic Civil Rights gains of the 1960s, and the establishment of the first affirmative action programs. Already by 1950, total skilled and unskilled blue-collar employment had risen to nearly 70 percent of black workers.

18. Billingsley, *Jacob's Ladder*, p. 138.

19. Gutman, p. 467, discusses that situation of blacks in the decades after the Great Depression. "Urban unemployment and underemployment greeted those driven from the land. The cities had too few jobs. A regular differential in the black–white unemployment rate (two-to-one) made adaptation to northern city life very difficult for migrant blacks, a point made by Daniel P. Moynihan but buried in the dispute over an alleged 'tangle of pathology.' 'The fundamental overwhelming fact is that Negro *unemployment*, with the exception of the few years during World War Two and the Korean War,' said Moynihan in 1965, 'has continued at disaster levels for thirty-five years.' " See also Mead, p. 101: "Marriage rates have plunged among black men, but this is true for successful and unsuccessful blacks alike. The unemployment rate shows little connection to whether black men become fathers or husbands. They appear to be having a much tougher time staying married than finding work."

20. Gutman, p. 525.

21. Ibid., p. 529.

22. Billingsley, *Black Families*, pp. 68–69.

23. Mellon, p. 29.

24. Blassingame, pp. 173–74.

25. Genovese, p. 453.

26. Gutman, p. 318.
27. Douglass, p. 96.
28. Blassingame, p. 297.
29. Frazier, p. 41.
30. Genovese, p. 451.
31. Blassingame, pp. 198–99.
32. Mellon, p. 15.
33. Blassingame, pp. 187–88.
34. Gutman, pp. xxii, xxiii.
35. E. Franklin Frazier, "Three Scourges of the Negro Family," as quoted in Platt, p. 139.
36. Genovese, p. 505.
37. Gutman, pp. 190–91. He rightly rejects the notion that these names were given by slaveholders; p. 194.
38. Blassingame, pp. 198–99.
39. Gutman, p. 203.
40. Ibid.

CHAPTER 3: THE LITTLE WHEEL RUN BY FAITH

1. Blassingame, p. 170.
2. Ira Berlin, p. 302.
3. Frazier, Negro Church, p. 40.
4. Staples and Johnson, p. 212.
5. Frazier, Negro Family. Frazier goes on to assert that "in those cases the discipline of the church did not appear as a very effective means of social control. As a rule, church discipline amounts to little more than a mere formality, although it may be supported by a genuinely strong sentiment on the part of few individual members." As we shall see later, Frazier has an unaccountably strong contempt for the black church. As we saw in the previous chapter, against all odds, the black community developed and maintained a marriage-based family structure, with the black church as almost its only external institutional support. This result suggests a fairly high degree of effectiveness.
6. Sterling Stuckey, p. 39.
7. Genovese, p. 197.
8. Ibid., p. 258. See also Blassingame, p. 131: "The true shepherd of the black flock was the slave preacher. Often one of the few slaves who could

read, the black preacher was usually highly intelligent, resourceful, and noted for his powerful imagination and memory."

9. Blassingame, p. 132.

10. On this point, see Berlin, p. 301: "White churchmen had hoped that the separate instruction of blacks would allow them to purge black religion of its distinctive style and content."

11. Herskovits, pp. 137–38.

12. Genovese, p. 236.

13. Blassingame, p. 131. Stuckey, p. 15, sees the preacher not just as a Christian figure, but as the reembodiment of the African priest: "Other African institutions and African priests were brought to America in large numbers and, unrecognized by whites, found their places in the circle and elsewhere. Some were among the first and last slave preachers." See also p. 38: "African religious leaders predominated in slavery and in that oppressive environment orchestrated their people's transformation into a single people culturally. James Weldon Johnson makes the penetrating observation that it was through the old Negro preacher that 'people of diverse languages and customs who were brought here from diverse parts of Africa and thrown into slavery were given their first sense of unity and solidarity' . . ." Stuckey's view echoes W.E.B. Du Bois's insightful discussion: "The chief remaining institution was the Priest or Medicine-man. He early appeared on the plantation and found his function as the healer of the sick, the interpreter of the unknown, the comforter of the sorrowing, the supernatural avenger of wrong, and the one who rudely but picturesquely expressed the longing, disappointment, and resentment of a stolen, oppressed people. Thus, as bard, physician, judge, and priest, within the narrow limits allowed by the slave system, rose the Negro preacher, and under him the first Afro-American institution, the Negro church. This church was not at first by any means Christian nor definitely organized; rather it was an adaptation and mingling of heathen rites among the members of each plantation, roughly designated as Voodooism. . . . After the lapse of many generations the Negro church became Christian." Du Bois, pp. 144–45.

14. Frazier, *Negro Church*, p. 25.

15. Ibid., Chapter 2. For a succinct discussion of this development, see also Berlin, pp. 70–78.

16. Frazier, p. 33.

17. Berlin, p. 71.

18. Ibid., p. 293. See also Franklin, p. 53: "There was great reluctance on the part of the slaveholders to allow the evangelization of the slaves."

19. Berlin, p. 297.

20. Ibid., p. 302.

21. Franklin, pp. 144–45. Yet later Franklin will acknowledge: "The socially active and culturally aware black church congregation embodied the predominant values that emerged from the Afro-American experience in the nineteenth century," and he declares the black church (along with the black press) a "central cultural institution" for Afro-Americans.

22. Even the great migration did not lead to a great decline in church membership. See Lincoln and Mamiya, p. 117.

23. See John H. Franklin, p. 321: "Although Garvey's claim that he had 4 million followers in 1920 and 6 million three years later is doubtless exaggerated, even his severest critics admitted that there were perhaps a half million members of the UNIA." By comparison, for example, the number of black American Baptists passed the half-million mark in 1870, and by 1915, there were 3 million members in the National Baptist Convention. Lincoln and Mamiya, pp. 25, 30.

24. Ibid., p. 8. This will be discussed in greater detail in the next chapter.

25. Frazier, *Negro Church*, p. 90.

26. The contradictory tendencies in enslaver views is well illustrated by a passage in Northup, p. 69. He describes his master's encouragement of Christianity among the slaves, and the impact of religion on Sam, one of his fellow bondsmen: "In the course of the summer Sam became deeply convicted, his mind dwelling intensely on the subject of religion. His mistress gave him a Bible, which he carried with him to his work. . . . Sam's piety was frequently observed by white men who came to the mill and the remark it most generally provoked was, that a man like Ford, who allowed his slaves to have Bibles, was 'not fit to own a nigger.' " See also Stuckey, pp. 37–38. For a general discussion of enslaver attitudes toward Christian conversion, see Genovese, pp. 183–93.

27. Lincoln and Mamiya, p. 6.

28. Frazier, *Negro Church*, p. 16.

29. Genovese, p. 233.

30. Ibid., pp. 243–44.

31. See Genovese's insightful discussion of the ethics and theology of religion among the enslaved, pp. 244–55.

32. Stuckey argues most effectively in favor of important African influ-

ences in the religion of the slaves. In addition to specific survivals in music and dance rituals, he cites African ideas of spirituality, priesthood, community—and of religion as an instrument and expression of communal needs. The entire first chapter of *Slave Culture* represents this view.

33. References to pagan and paganism in the text are not intended in any pejorative sense, but as a convenient way of referring to religions that stand outside the monotheistic, biblical, or Koranic tradition that is to a degree shared by Christianity, Judaism, and Islam.

34. Historically, Christianity had a subversive and eventually overpowering effect on the societies where it took strongest root. Gibbon, the famed English chronicler of Rome's decline and fall, was not entirely mistaken when he ascribed the collapse of ancient Rome to Christianity's adverse effect on the moral and political culture that fostered and sustained Roman imperialism. The destructive religious wars that ravaged Europe for the better part of two centuries also had something to do with the potentially all-consuming moral imperatives of Christian doctrine. The clear distinction in modern Western thought between the sacred and the secular, the realm of religion and that of the state, owes its origins largely to the intellectual and moral reaction against those religious wars. Political and religious thinkers saw the need to disentangle the political and religious sources of authority, in an effort to avoid the combustible mixture of faith with armed forced, of righteous zeal with worldly self-interest.

35. For a succinct discussion of the religious hypocrisy of the enslavers, and its effect on the enslaved, see V. P. Franklin, pp. 55–57.

36. Blassingame, pp. 130–31: "Most slaves, repelled by the brand of religion their masters taught, the racial inequalities in white churches, and the limitations on the bondsmen's autonomy, formulated new ideas and practices in the quarters."

37. From "Bishop Daniel Alexander Payne's Protestation of American Slavery," as quoted in Cone, p. 63. In this context, Payne says that such cynicism led some enslaved people to turn against all religion, and question the existence of God. See also V. P. Franklin, pp. 54, 66–67.

38. V. P. Franklin, pp. 61–62. He goes on to describe the account of a black preacher who was "burnt alive within one mile of the court-house at Greenville" for refusing to cease his preaching. On the general point under discussion, see Blassingame, pp. 310–11.

39. See Genovese, pp. 6–7, who argues that blacks "by accepting a paternalistic ethos and legitimizing class rule, developed their most powerful

defense against the dehumanization implicit in slavery." He then goes on to observe that "the slave, drawing on a religion that was supposed to assure their compliance and docility, rejected the essence of slavery by projecting their own rights and value as human beings." Unfortunately, he does not think through the content of Christian doctrine sufficiently to see that these statements are contradictory.

40.   "Except as ye be converted, and become as little children, ye shall not enter into the kingdom of heaven. Whosoever, therefore, shall humble himself as this little child, the same is greatest in the kingdom of heaven. . . . But whoso shall offend one of these little ones which believe in me, it were better for him that a millstone were hanged about his neck, and that he were drowned in the depths of the sea" (Matthew 18:3–6). Lincoln appreciated the importance of this passage in understanding the moral significance of the slavery issue during the Civil War. In his second inaugural address, he culminates his discussion of the causes of the war with Matthew 18:7—"Woe unto the world because of offenses! for it must needs be that offenses come; but woe to that man by whom the offense cometh." Also cp. Martin Delany's use in the antislavery context of Christ's doctrine of the special status of children: "That his [the colored man's] cause was the cause of God—that 'Inasmuch as ye did it not unto the least of these my little ones, ye did it not unto me' . . ." From "The Condition, Elevation, Emigration and Destiny of the Colored People of the United States," in Brotz, ed., p. 45.

41.   Solomon Northup's summary account of life in subjection to Edwin Epps perfectly illustrates the slave's plight. Epps would beat his slaves for inadequate work. He would demand that they dance and revel at his whim. In drunken sport, he would lash whichever slave came within his reach: Northup, pp. 136–39. But the plight of one female slave epitomizes the slave's helpless degradation: "She had a genial and pleasant temper, and was faithful and obedient. . . . Her back bore the scars of a thousand stripes; not because she was of an unmindful and rebellious spirit, but because it had fallen to her lot to be the slave of a licentious master and a jealous mistress. She shrank before the lustful eye of the one, and was in danger even of her life at the hands of the other, and between the two, she was indeed accursed. The enslaved victim of lust and hate, Patsey had no comfort of her life." Ibid., p. 143.

42.   This view has long been held against Christianity in general. Consider, for example, John Stuart Mill's (p. 90) description of Christianity:

"It is essentially a doctrine of passive obedience; it inculcates submission to all authorities found established; who indeed are not to be actively obeyed when they command what religion forbids, but who are not to be resisted, far less rebelled against, for any amount of wrong to ourselves." Mill ascribes to Christianity "a standard of ethics in which the only worth, professedly recognized, is that of obedience." It's ironic that the great defender of human liberty fell prey to the same willful misunderstanding of Christian ethics as the enslavers of humanity.

43. V. P. Franklin, p. 47.

44. As V. P. Franklin, p. 74, observes, in the course of citing several examples: ". . . the act of resistance was an act of self-definition and self-respect."

45. "The religion practiced in the quarters gave the slaves the one thing they absolutely had to have if they were to resist being transformed into the Sambos they had been programmed to become. It fired them with a sense of their own worth before God and man. It enabled them to prove to themselves, and to a world that never ceased to need reminding, that no man's will can become that of another unless he himself wills it—that the ideal of slavery cannot be realized, no matter how badly the body is broken and the spirit tormented." Genovese, p. 283.

46. Cone, p. 93.

47. Ibid., p. 86.

48. Ibid., p. 95.

49. V. P. Franklin, p. 60.

50. Cone, p. 76.

51. Ibid.

52. Blassingame, p. 133.

53. Ibid., p. 129.

54. V. P. Franklin points out that "slave letters, narratives, and interviews are filled with statements about God's justice v. the evil slaveholder." He goes on to cite numerous examples.

55. This kind of error is in general one of the pitfalls in the path of Afrocentric thinking. As I have said elsewhere: "Works produced in reaction against demeaning racial stereotypes begin by accepting race or skin color as their analytical category. The author then searches through history looking for examples that fall within this category. Whatever the results, the work remains within the confines of the original racial category. Like someone struggling in quicksand, the researcher's efforts to struggle

against racism simply involve him more deeply in its worldview." From "Heroic Fulfillment Closer to Home," *The Washington Times*, June 6, 1993, p. G-2. To avoid this pitfall, we must learn from the wisdom of the enslaved, and seek a transcendent basis for our identity that is independent of the racist categories of the dialectic of oppression.

56. This implication Christianizes an aspect of religious power in the African tradition. For example, the insurrectionary Denmark Vesey worked with an African nicknamed Gullah Jack who distributed charms to Vesey's adherents "consisting of parched corn and ground nuts, and said eat that and nothing else on the morning it breaks out . . . and you can't be wounded. . . ." Christianity has a charm that promises less and yet more. Death isn't avoided, but its meaning is overcome. The body doesn't escape it, but the mind and heart may be freed from its overawing power.

57. On the role of religion and the Bible in the slave insurrections, see Blassingame, p. 221; Bennet, pp. 111, 113–14, 118–19; Stuckey, p. 52; Genovese, pp. 593–94; Lincoln and Mamiya, p. 203.

58. Bennett, p. 144, says that "Sojourner Truth and Harriet Tubman had staying power. Both were fanatically religious, but they expressed their religion in different ways." See also Stuckey, pp. 194–95; Lincoln and Mamiya, p. 282.

59. Blassingame, p. 221.

60. Lincoln and Mamiya, p. 202.

61. Du Bois, pp. 146, 147.

62. Bernard Mays, *The Negro's God as Reflected in His Literature*, as quoted in V. P. Franklin, p. 32.

63. The French philosopher Montaigne aptly translates this ancient Roman sentiment: "The contemplation of death is the contemplation of liberty. He who has learned to die, has forgotten how to be enslaved." *Essays*, I, XXII.

64. Aristotle, pp. 14–16.

CHAPTER 4: THOSE WHO WOULD BE FREE

1. See, for example, the proslavery arguments cited in Berlin, pp. 87–88; Tise, pp. 107–9.

2. For a good general overview of this point, see Genovese, pp. 561–66. To illustrate the self-contradictory character of the enslavers' views of black potential, he reports a comment by Fanny Kemble, an exceptionally honest

white observer: "If they are incapable of profiting by instruction, I do not see the necessity for laws inflicting heavy penalties on those who offer it to them. . . . We have no laws forbidding us to teach our dogs and horses as much as they can comprehend."

3. Brotz, ed., p. 217. Douglass goes on to declare: "The great mass of slaveholders look upon education among the slaves as utterly subversive of the slave system."

4. Ibid., p. 563.

5. V. P. Franklin, pp. 161–62.

6. Blassingame, p. 312.

7. Ibid., p. 164.

8. V. P. Franklin, p. 163.

9. Berlin, pp. 303–304.

10. J. H. Franklin, p. 149.

11. Berlin, p. 304.

12. Ibid., pp. 305–306. On public sentiment in the South against education for free Negroes, see also J. H. Franklin, p. 148.

13. V. P. Franklin, p. 173.

14. Ibid., p. 175.

15. Ibid.

16. Ibid., p. 176.

17. Fogel and Engerman, p. 261.

18. Ibid., p. 263.

19. The best summary of Washington's philosophy, in his own words, is in the speech he delivered to the Atlanta Exposition in September, 1895. See Brotz, ed., pp. 351–463, for an excellent sampling of Washington's views. For an analysis of the historical background of Washington's philosophy, and his differences with Du Bois, see Meier, and also Brotz, ed., pp. 12–24.

20. Abernathy, Chapter 1. See also Du Bois, pp. 55–64.

21. Washington summarized his view of the increase in black owners, managers, and tenant farmers after the Civil War in *The Negro in Business*, published in 1907. "Practically all of the Negro owners of farms have become owners since 1860; in that year the Negro was landless. In the South Central States since 1860 Negro farmers have come to operate as owners and managers 95,624 farms and as tenants 348,805. The farms operated by owners or managers are thus 21.5 percent of the total." He goes on to say that in the South Atlantic States, between 1860 and 1900

"287,933 Negroes had acquired control of farmland in these states of whom 202,578 or 70.4 percent were tenants and 85,355 or 29.6 percent were owners or managers." As quoted in Brotz, ed., p. 400.

22. Meier, Chapter IX.

23. Brotz, ed., p. 221.

24. Ibid.

25. Ibid., p. 224.

26. Ibid., p. 504.

27. Duberman, p. 55. Many years before Robeson's difficulties, Frederick Douglass summarized the plight of highly educated blacks in a letter to Harriet Beecher Stowe. "White people will not employ them to the obvious embarrassment of their causes, and the blacks, taking their cue from the whites, have not sufficient confidence in their abilities to employ them. Hence, educated colored men, among the colored people, are at a very great discount." Brotz, ed., p. 222.

28. Consider, for example, what Brotz, ed., says of Du Bois (p. 21), in comparison with Frederick Douglass or Booker T. Washington: ". . . Du Bois was much more humiliated by racialist theories than either of his two great predecessors. Perhaps because they had both come 'up from slavery,' Douglass and Washington had inner resources which made them much more independent than Du Bois of white opinion or any opinion. . . . Du Bois . . . moved in a world in which, to exaggerate only somewhat, he felt that every white person regarded him as inferior because of his Negro 'blood.' Reacting to this with resentment, he plunged into an attack on racialism. But, as is often the case, he became imprisoned by the assumptions of the very people he was attacking."

29. Du Bois goes so far as to say that "we must lay on the soul of this man a heavy responsibility for the consummation of Negro disenfranchisement, the decline of the Negro college and public school and the firmer establishment of color caste in this land." Given that all these things were the result of a white racist agenda of repression, which no one believes blacks at the time could have forestalled, this has to be the first example of what would later be derided as "blaming the victim." See Brotz, ed., pp. 15–16, where he points out that Washington was "the de facto leader of the opinion in the South, white as well as black, which opposed disenfranchisement," but that "he thought it would not stop the progress which the Negro in his condition of partial freedom, had made since emancipation and would continue to make."

30. See especially Du Bois, Essay "Of Booker T. Washington and Others," pp. 42–54. In a letter to Miss A. P. Moore, Du Bois summarizes his differences with Washington succinctly: "We did not object to industrial education, we did not object to his enthusiasm for its advancement, we did object to his attacks upon higher training and upon his general attitude of belittling the race and of not putting enough stress upon voting and things of that sort." See "Letter to Miss Moore" in Hamilton, ed., p. 73.

31. Ibid., p. 50.

32. Du Bois, p. 49.

33. Hamilton, ed., pp. 65–66.

34. Brotz, ed., p. 21: "To Du Bois, for example, a primary cause of slavery or of disenfranchisement was a doctrine or an 'ism' postulating the inferiority of the Negro. Hence to change the power pattern one had to change the doctrine by disseminating a counter doctrine."

35. Hamilton, ed., pp. 149–50.

36. Lomax, pp. 20–21.

37. Ibid., p. 202.

38. Ibid., p. 206.

39. Ibid., p. 214.

40. Ibid., p. 220.

41. Ibid., p. 221.

42. I elaborate on the tragic consequences of this error in the chapter entitled "Not by Bread Alone."

43. Du Bois, pp. 16–17: It is a tribute to Du Bois's resonant insight into the black-American psyche that very few people who have written about our experience since he did have been able to avoid citing or alluding to this paragraph at some point in their writing.

44. Ibid., pp. 200–201.

CHAPTER 5: THAT'S GOT HIS OWN

1. Brotz, ed., p. 204.

2. Ibid., p. 54.

3. Ibid., p. 503.

4. Ibid., p. 553.

5. Ibid., p. 564.

6. Hamilton, ed., p. 148.

7. Bennett, p. 296.

8. Essien-Udom, p. 39.

9. Bennett, pp. 295–96; J. H. Franklin, pp. 320–22.

10. Meier, p. 124.

11. Brotz, ed., p. 566.

12. The reader should note that I use the word *foundation* advisedly. A foundation is a basis and starting point for development, not the ultimate goal. No black leaders predicated black economic advancement on the exclusive exploitation of opportunities in the black community. Even the separatists and nationalists, who advocated colonization or a separate state, envisaged participation in the international economy.

13. In discussing the National Negro Business League, Meier alludes to this "definite dualism," saying, "It asserted that the economic laws of laissez faire were blind to color differences and that economic usefulness and success were the best way to eliminate prejudice, but it also vigorously propagandized for Negro support for Negro business." Meier, p. 125.

14. Ibid., p. 147.

15. Meier, p. 130.

16. Ibid., pp. 130–33, on the role of the church as an economic and social-welfare institution; also Frazier, *Negro Church*, p. 88.

17. Meier, p. 134.

18. Frazier, *Negro Church*, p. 49.

19. Unfortunately, here again Frazier observed the facts without understanding them, because he remained trapped in the racial dialectic. Thus he saw church political activities as an emotional release, vicarious participation in the "real" politics of the white-dominated world from which racism banished blacks. This meant that he did not take them seriously as what they were—the black community's· means of self-government, camouflaged in clerical garb.

20. On the concept of charismatic leadership and its influence see Bloom, pp. 211–13.

21. At the first mass meeting during the Montgomery bus boycott, King reminded his audience that "Love is one of the pinnacle parts of the Christian faith. There is another side called justice. And justice is really love in calculation." Garrow, p. 24.

22. Washington, ed., p. 9.

23. Ibid., pp. 13–14.

24. Ibid., p. 18.

25. Ibid., p. 6.

26. Ibid., pp. 17–18.
27. Ibid., pp. 32–33.
28. Ibid., p. 12.
29. Ibid., p. 39.

CHAPTER 6: OF JESSE JACKSON AND OTHERS

1. Simson, p. 637.
2. Weiss, p. 39: "By contrast it was absolutely vital for the President to respond to the concerns of the southern senators and congressmen who could determine the fate of his legislative program. Not only was the new Vice-President a southerner; so were the majority leaders of the House and Senate and the chairmen of the major congressional committees. Roosevelt needed their votes to put through what he regarded as 'must' recovery legislation, and he was unwilling to risk alienating them by championing racial causes"; cf. p. 106. See also Raymond Walters, "The New Deal and the Negro," in Braeman et al., eds., p. 200; and Harvard Sitkoff, "The Impact of the New Deal on Black Southerners," in Cobb and Namorato, eds., p. 118.
3. In Ibid., p. 118, Sitkoff observes that the New Deal "left southern blacks at the mercy of those planters, industrialists, union chieftains and political officeholders who stood to profit the most by continuing to oppress Afro-Americans. Those who made the decisions at the local level made sure black Southerners never shared fully or fairly in the material benefits of the New Deal."
4. Weiss, p. 59. See also Walters in Braeman et al., eds., pp. 186–89.
5. Ibid., p. 55. Part of the decline in white sharecroppers may have been due to racial bias, i.e., white sharecroppers "promoted" to tenant status at the expense of blacks who were pushed off the land. See also, Walters, in Braeman et al., eds., pp. 171–75.
6. Ibid., p. 54; cp. Walters, in Braeman et al., eds., p. 191. The CCC was headed by Robert Fechner, a bigoted white from Tennessee and a "prominent official in the racially exclusionist International Association of Machinists." It took three years for black enrollment to reach a point that reflected the black proportion of the population. It never reflected the black population's disproportionate participation in the nation's economic misery.
7. See J. H. Franklin, p. 354: "There was a greater inclination toward

fairness to Negroes in providing relief than in providing employment." See also Sitkoff in Cobb and Namorato, ed., p. 123.

8. Anderson, pp. 241–61.

9. Weiss, p. 178. See also Walters in Braeman et al., eds., p. 210, concerning the warnings of Professor Newell D. Eason of Shaw University. He predicted that relief would pauperize the race by inculcating a certain contempt for work and a willingness "to cling to the minimum existence which seems to be guaranteed by the relief agency."

10. Anderson, p. 241.

11. Weiss, p. 166.

12. Sitkoff in Cobb and Namorato, eds., pp. 120–21.

13. Weiss, Chapter VI.

14. Ibid., Chapter X and Sitkoff, in Cobb and Namorato, eds., pp. 128–32.

15. Ibid., p. 21: "As late as 1940, out of a potential black electorate of more than 4.2 million in the old Confederacy, only 200,000—less than 5 percent—were even registered to vote. Those blacks who resided elsewhere—2.1 million twenty-one years of age or older in 1930, 2.4 million in 1940—constituted less than 3 percent of the potential national electorate."

16. Yet when the returns came in, "Negroes defected in smaller numbers in the 1932 election than did any other group of Republican voters": Samuel Lubell, "The Negro and the Democratic Coalition," *Commentary*, Aug. 1964, as quoted in Weiss, p. 29.

17. Weiss, p. xv: "Two thirds of blacks of voting age in the 1930s lived in the old Confederacy and in the District of Columbia; for the most part, this meant that they were unable to vote."

18. For a detailed account of King's Chicago effort, see Garrow, chapters 8, 9.

19. See the description of views on the background of the Johnson administration antipoverty campaign in Mark I. Gelfand, "The War on Poverty," in Divine, ed., Vol. 1, pp. 128–29.

20. Ibid., pp. 136–37.

21. Moynihan, *Misunderstanding*, pp. 130–31.

22. Ibid., pp. 134–35.

23. Ibid., pp. 135–36.

24. According to the 1990 U. S. Census, blacks are twice as likely to work for the federal government as whites. Employment at all levels of

government accounts for nearly a quarter (22.8 percent) of black employment, as opposed to just 15 percent for whites. Source: "The Black Population in the United States": March 1991, *Current Population Reports*, P20-464.

25.   On Jackson's career, see Landess and Quinn.

26.   Senator Carol Moseley Braun of Illinois is withholding her support because the FOCA bill perpetuates restrictions of use of federal funds to finance abortions for the poor. She is staunchly in favor of unlimited access to abortions.

27.   A poll in *The Boston Globe*, March 31, 1989, for example, reported that 48 percent of blacks said that abortion should not be legal under any circumstances, 42 percent that it should only be legal in certain instances. That makes 90 percent opposed to legalized abortion in all or some cases. The comparable figure for whites was 73 percent.

28.   Letter to Clarence Gamble, Oct. 19, 1939. Sanger manuscripts, Sophia Smith Collection, Smith College.

29.   Author of the racist tract *The Rising Tide of Color Against White World-Supremacy*.

30.   This legislation, strongly supported by organized labor, prohibits employers from hiring permanent replacements for striking workers. Though it aims to protect employed, unionized workers, it eliminates opportunities for the unemployed, among whom blacks are disproportionately represented.

CHAPTER 7: NOT BY BREAD ALONE

1.   Mead, p. 143, 144.

2.   Staples and Johnson, p. 73: "The diversity of African cultures precludes any generalizations about African sexual behavior. But in the past, African sex life could only be understood in relation to the kinship groups, which provided the basis of the mores and folkways that regulated sexual relations. . . . The violation of sexual laws is an offense against individuals and not against God."

3.   Ibid.: "All the available evidence indicates that sexual behavior in Africa before and after marriage was under strict community and family control."

4.   See Lemann. Ironically, his essential negative portrayal of black family

values serves to illustrate this point. Lemann writes that one Ruby Daniels, whose life exemplifies the pattern of illegitimacy and family breakdown, constantly strives to achieve a lasting marriage. Though she fails repeatedly, it is clear that she is responding to a strong cultural ideal.

5. I wonder if Mead realizes that this is just a fancy way of saying that blacks are lazy and don't like to work.

6. Mead seems unaware of the great exodus from the lower South to the Midwest (mainly Kansas) that occurred at the beginning of the 1880s. See Gutman, pp. 433–41, who notes that "migration had been and would remain a central social experience among Afro-Americans." He points out that even those who did not join in the great exodus often shared the dissatisfaction of those who migrated.

7. Mead, p. 149. Aside from ignoring the now well-documented history of black efforts to achieve both psychological and economic autonomy, Mead's too-facile account seems to imply that slavery was just an experience of prejudice, rather than a totalitarian system of economic exploitation, maintained by physical violence and ruthless psychological warfare. He also writes as if blacks were simply free agents after Emancipation, entirely ignoring the comprehensive regime of political disenfranchisement, economic manipulation, and physical violence, amounting in some cases to virtual reenslavement, which whites employed to control black behavior.

8. Ibid., p. 148.

9. Lincoln and Mamiya, p. 382.

10. Lemann, p. 28.

11. Ibid., pp. 28–31.

12. Ibid.

13. Gutman, p. 433.

14. Gutman, p. 456.

15. Moynihan, *Negro Family*, Chapter 2, p. 34.

16. Mead, p. 253.

17. Lemann, pp. 350–51.

18. For a detailed, firsthand account of subjection to the welfare system, see Funiciello, especially Chapter 2.

19. I don't mean to criticize reforms that tie welfare help to some work requirement. I do believe that such requirements could become part of an oppressive regime if administered by large, impersonal bureaucracies.

20. Murray, p. 162.

21. In his short story "The City of Refuge," published in 1924, Rudolph Fisher penned a passage that poignantly captures this phenomenon. A black recently arrived in Harlem from the South is describing white harassment of blacks back in North Carolina. "Know whut dey done? Dey killed five o' Mose Joplin's hawses 'fo he lef'. Put groun' glass in de feed-trough. Sam Cheevers come up on three of 'em one night pizenin' his well. Bleesom beat Crinshaw out o' sixty acres o' lan' an' a year's crops. Dass jess how 't is. Soon's a nigger make a li'l sump'n he better git to leavin'." Clarke, ed., p. 25.

CHAPTER 8: RENEWING THE FOUNDATIONS

1. "There are countries in Europe where the inhabitant feels like some sort of farm laborer indifferent to the fate of the place where he dwells. The greatest changes may take place in his country without his concurrence; he does not even know precisely what has happened; he is in doubt; he has heard tell by chance of what goes on. Worse still, the condition of his village, the policing of his road, and the repair of his church and parsonage do not concern him; he thinks that all those things have nothing to do with him at all, but belong to a powerful stranger called the government. For his part, he enjoys what he has as a tenant, without feeling of ownership or any thought of improvement. His detachment from his own fate goes so far that if his own safety or that of his children is in danger, instead of trying to ward the peril off, he crosses his arms and waits for the whole nation to come to his aid. Furthermore, this man who has so completely sacrificed his freedom of will does not like obedience more than the next man. He submits, it is true, to the caprice of a clerk, but as soon as force is withdrawn, he will vaunt his triumph over the law as over a conquered foe. Thus he oscillates the whole time between servility and license." Tocqueville, pp. 93–94.

2. This discussion of school choice is not intended to be comprehensive or complete, only suggestive. Any actual school-choice proposal has to be devised to suit the circumstances and needs of the communities involved. The society obviously also has an interest in making sure that certain subjects (American history, for example) and certain values (like citizenship) are presented in a reasonably consistent way in all the nation's

schools. This suggests the need for periodic, grade-appropriate standardized tests in certain core areas (for example, reading, math, American history, and science at the elementary level) to make sure every school is in fact achieving results for its students that meet or surpass a certain threshold level of educational performance.

BIBLIOGRAPHY

BOOKS

Abernathy, Ralph D. *And the Walls Came Tumbling Down.* New York: Harper & Row, 1989.

Anderson, Jervis. *A. Philip Randolph.* New York: Harcourt Brace Jovanovich, 1973.

Aristotle. *Politics.* Cambridge, Mass.: Harvard University Press, 1967.

Bennett, Lerone, Jr. *Before the Mayflower.* Baltimore: Penguin Books, 1966.

Berlin, Ira. *Slaves Without Masters.* New York: Oxford University Press, 1981.

Billingsley, Andrew. *Black Families in White America.* New York: Touchstone, 1988.

————. *Climbing Jacob's Ladder.* New York: Simon & Schuster, 1992.

Blassingame, John W. *The Slave Community.* New York: Oxford University Press, 1979.

Bloom, Allan. *The Closing of the American Mind*. New York: Simon & Schuster, 1987.

Braeman, John, et al. *The New Deal*. Columbus: Ohio State University Press, 1975.

Brotz, Howard. *Negro Social and Political Thought*. New York: Basic Books, 1966.

Clarke, John H. *A Century of the Best Black American Short Stories*. New York: Hill & Wang, 1993.

Cobb, James C. *The New Deal and the South*. Jackson: University Press of Mississippi, 1984.

Cone, James H. *The Spirituals and the Blues*. Maryknoll, N.Y.: Orbis Books, 1991.

Douglass, Frederick. *The Life and Times of Frederick Douglass*. New York: Bonanza Books, 1962.

Duberman, Martin B. *Paul Robeson*. New York: Alfred A. Knopf, 1989.

Du Bois, W.E.B. *The Souls of Black Folk*. New York: Fawcett Publications, 1961.

Essien-Udom, E. U. *Black Nationalism*. Chicago: The University of Chicago Press, 1962.

Fogel, Robert W., and Stanley L. Engerman. *Time on the Cross*. New York: W. W. Norton & Company, 1989.

Franklin, John H. *From Slavery to Freedom*. New York: Alfred A. Knopf, 1988.

Franklin, V. P. *Black Self-Determination*. Brooklyn, N.Y.: Laurence Hill Books, 1992.

Frazier, E. Franklin. *The Negro Church in America*. New York: Schocken Books, 1974.

―――. *The Negro Family in the United States*. Chicago: The University of Chicago Press, 1966.

Funiciello, Theresa. *Tyranny of Kindness*. New York: The Atlantic Monthly Press, 1993.

Garrow, David J. *Bearing the Cross*. New York: Vintage Books, 1988.

Genovese, Eugene D. *Roll, Jordan, Roll*. New York: Vintage Books, 1975.

Gutman, Herbert G. *The Black Family in Slavery and Freedom*. New York: Vintage Books, 1977.

Hacker, Andrew. *Two Nations*. New York: Ballantine Books, 1992.

Hamilton, Virginia. *The Writings of W.E.B. Dubois*. New York: Thomas Y. Crowell Co., 1975.

Herskovits, Melville J. *The Myth of the Negro Past*. Boston: Beacon Press, 1990.

Landess, Thomas. *Jesse Jackson and the Politics of Race*. Ottawa, Ill.: Jameson Books, 1985.

Lemann, Nicholas. *The Promised Land*. New York: Vintage Books, 1992.

Levine, Lawrence W. *Black Culture and Black Consciousness*. New York: Oxford University Press, 1977.

Lincoln, C. E. *The Black Church in the African American Experience*. Durham, N.C.: Duke University Press, 1990.

———. *The Black Church Since Frazier*. New York: Schocken Books, 1974.

Livy. *The Early History of Rome*. Baltimore: Penguin Books, 1971.

Lomax, Louis E. *The Negro Revolt*. New York: The New American Library, 1963.

Mays, Benjamin E. *The Negro's God as Reflected in His Literature*. New York: Atheneum, 1968.

Mead, Lawrence M. *The New Politics of Poverty*. New York: Basic Books, 1992.

Meier, August. *Negro Thought in America*. Ann Arbor, Mich.: Ann Arbor Paperbacks, 1988.

Mellon, James, ed. *Bullwhip Days*. New York: Avon Books, 1988.

Mill, John S. *On Liberty*. New York: The Classics of Liberty Library, 1992.

Montaigne, Michel de. *Oeuvres Complètes*. Paris: Gallimard, 1962.

Moynihan, Daniel P. *Maximum Feasible Misunderstanding*. New York: The Free Press, 1970.

Murray, Charles. *Losing Ground*. New York: Basic Books, 1984.

Northup, Solomon. *Twelve Years a Slave*. Baton Rouge: Louisiana State University Press, 1989.

Platt, Anthony M. *E. Franklin Frazier Reconsidered*. New Brunswick, N.J.: Rutgers University Press, 1991.

Scanzoni, John H. *The Black Family in Modern Society*. Chicago: The University of Chicago Press, 1977.

Staples, Robert. *Black Families at the Crossroads*. San Francisco: Jossey-Bass, Inc., 1993.

Stuckey, Sterling. *Slave Culture*. New York: Oxford University Press, 1987.

Tise, Larry E. *Proslavery*. Athens: The University of Georgia Press, 1987.

Tocqueville, Alexis de. *Democracy in America*. Garden City, N.Y.: Anchor Books, 1969.

Washington, Kames M. *A Testament of Hope*. San Francisco: Harper & Row, 1986.

Weiss, Nancy J. *Farewell to the Party of Lincoln*. Princeton, N.J.: Princeton University Press, 1983.

Wilson, William J. *The Declining Significance of Race*. Chicago: The University of Chicago Press, 1980.

Woodson, Carter G. *The Miseducation of the Negro*. Trenton, N.J.: Africa World Press, Inc., 1990.

Woodward, C. V. *The Strange Career of Jim Crow*. London: Oxford University Press, 1974.

ARTICLES

Simson, Gary J. "Thomas Supreme Unfitness": *Cornell Law Review*, 1991.

INDEX